Matrix Messiah

DYLAN MORRISON

Matrix Messiah
ISBN-13: 978-1500879594
ISBN-10: 1500879592

Copyright © 2014 Dylan Morrison

The right of Dylan Morrison to be identified as the author of this work has been asserted in accordance with sections 77 and 78 of the Copyright, Designs and Patents Act 1988.

The cover image is the copyright of David Hayward, 2014. All rights are reserved.

The cover design is the copyright of Ping Creative Ltd 2014. All rights are reserved.

Matrix Messiah is published by Dylan Morrison Publishing.

To my Soul Mate, Zan, my companion in the Queendom for the last 34 years.

CONTENTS

	Acknowledgments	i
	Prologue	v
1	Model Obstacles	1
2	I Wanna Be Like You	7
3	Copy Cats	13
4	You, Me And Gravity	18
5	Cultural Band-Aids	25
6	Religion	32
7	I Don't Like To Judge, But …..	38
8	Feelings	43
9	New World Waiting	50
10	The Man From Beyond	54
11	Crossed Out	59
12	You Can't Keep A Good Man Down	64
13	The Empire Strikes Back	69
14	Red Or Blue Pill?	75
15	Contrasting Queendom	85
16	"Earth Calling Heaven!"	90
17	The Yeshua Prayer	95
18	The Spirit-Soul Reunion Waltz	103
19	Helper Or Healer?	109
20	Divine Resonance	114

21	The Walking Wounded	123
	Epilogue	131
	Glossary	134
	About The Author	139

Acknowledgements

Many of my fellow travellers have helped *Matrix Messiah* see the light of publication. Zan, my wife, best friend and oft-times psycho-spiritual adviser, continues to be an inspiration to me, as she presses on in her own liberating journey of self-discovery. Her many hours of dog sitting and coffee making have enabled me to retreat to the inner sanctum of study, where this material first flowed onto my laptop screen.

I wish to thank all those *new* friends that I've met on social media sites over the last few years, for their interest in what I have to say. The enriching collage of their spiritual and religious paradigms has inspired me to think further out of the Yeshua box than I would have previously dared. Our common desire to find the Love behind it all, has joined us in a most wonderful way.

From time to time, Divine Source brings along an individual who turns up at exactly the right time in our lives. One such human *angel* was the late Roel Kaptein, who introduced me to the writings of the French anthropological philosopher **René** Girard. Roel's wise council and Girard's *mimetic theory of human relationships* both proved lifesavers as I left behind the abusive fundamentalist religion of my youth. Thank you gentlemen for your courage in speaking out against the prevailing, status quo wisdom of our current age.

I'd also like to thank my counsellor friend, Anne Crawford, who introduced me to *psychosynthesis*, the therapeutic model of the late, Italian psychologist, Roberto Assagioli. Once more, a case of being brought to the right person, at the right time. Thank you Anne for your empathy and compassion. You are a true channel of psycho-spiritual healing and a wee gem of a person.

David Hayward, the supremely talented, Canadian artist responsible for cover art of this edition, has once again captured the essential spirit of my mystical musings. May I encourage you to pop over and have a wee look at David's prophetic art work online. You will be surprised at how often he hits the nail of religious scapegoating on the head. Thank you, David, for allowing your work to grace the cover of *Matrix Messiah*.

Thanks also to my friend Wayne Lockwood of Ping Creative Ltd. here in Lincoln, for his wonderful cover design skills. A sci-fi fan, he immediately came up with the look that I wanted, viz. one to highlight David's telling artwork and spark my readers' curiosity.

Finally, dear bookworms, I thank *you* for taking a

chance on this little publication. I sincerely believe that, read with an open heart, it may open you up to a new Reality, the matrix-free zone of the Queendom; that transcendent-immanent hiding place of Divine Love, the One without rivalry and violence.

Dylan Morrison
Lincoln, England
September 2014

Prologue

I've read a lot of books in my time, mostly those dealing with the timeless mystery of human existence; the mystery that inspires all the usual big questions. How come we're here? Why can life be so wonderful and yet so deeply tragic? Where will we all end up anyway? Now, as a somewhat naïve, young Irishman, I plumped for meaning in the evangelical Christianity of my Ulster homeland. There, the followers of Jesus came in all shapes and sizes, adhering to a mixed bag of dogmatic, theological beliefs. My tribe of choice quickly became the fledgling Charismatic movement, with its exuberant worship, speaking in tongues and prayer for healing. Gifted with a measure of revelatory insight, I soon slotted into the role of prophet, albeit a very minor one, within the hierarchical Shepherding movement of the late 70s and early 80s. Jesus, or Yeshua as I now prefer to call Him, was my hero, the revolutionary preacher-prophet who turned over tables and raised the dead.

I might still be a member of that zealous band of brothers if the unexpected hadn't happened. The sudden death of my infant son Ben back in 1984, threw a major curve ball in my direction. It signalled the beginning of an extended cold turkey experience; a withdrawal from my religious drug of choice, viz. church obsession.

Tottering towards the exit, I providentially bumped into the elderly, Dutch pastor and clinical psychologist, Roel Kaptein. A genuine guy who clearly loved Jesus, Roel was different from all the other supposed *men of God* who'd crossed my path in my Charismatic incarnation. He seemed somehow egoless and extremely full of common sense. To cut a long story short, Roel was able to identify and explain the inner angst that I'd been carrying around during my years of religious addiction. I was a casualty of *mimetic desire;* a powerful fascination that locks us into a see-saw, adoration-conflict scenario with our fellow man. Instantly, Roel's pinpoint diagnosis of my troubled, religious psyche lifted a weight off my dutiful shoulders. I was now free to rediscover my *Self;* an exploratory journey that would last for the next seventeen years. Yet, all through that period, Roel's incisive words of wisdom continued to echo around the chambers of my mind. *"Dylan, the power of the Fascination is always strong within us. Take care!"*

In June 2004, Divine Love decided that my time of soul-searching was up. Much to my surprise and without any prior permission, it's overpowering, yet deeply respectful Presence, elected to invade me. My original love for the Nazarene, was instantaneously reignited, though thankfully not in its previous evangelical manifestation. Instead, I was lifted onto a new Way, one that seemed to respect and complement my recent psycho-spiritual pilgrimage, with all its various highs and lows. I no longer carried with me the gut-gnawing feeling that something wasn't quite right with my take on Truth. Now, I felt an inner contentment, a serene sense of Divine acceptance, for perhaps the first time in my spiritual sojourn. Even my inner demons, those little footsoldiers of my ego army, sensed that something was different, that their days of psychic warfare had unexpectedly come to an end.

The result of this Divine hijacking has been the call to write; a summons to proclaim the unconditional nature of Divine Love by passing on the painful, yet liberating lessons that I've learnt along the way. Such lessons include those nuggets of wisdom dropped into by lap by Roel. Also in my psycho-spiritual treasure trove are the gems gleaned from the pioneering work of French anthropological philosopher, *René Girard*, the proposer of *mimetic theory*. These two men, along with *Roberto Assagioli,* the late, Italian transpersonal psychologist, have significantly shaped my spirituality and hence the work you are about to read. I humbly offer it to you for your consideration, trusting that it will enhance your view of the Nazarene and His psycho-spiritual keys for navigating this *desire matrix*, the illusory base camp that we call *life*.

Dylan Morrison
Lincoln, England
September 2014

1

Model Obstacles

We humans swim around in a sea of desire, believing ourselves to be the autonomous masters of our individual search for love. However, nothing could be further from the truth. In reality, we're splashing around in an ocean of *others*, who, like us, believe themselves to be self-governing seekers of Ultimate Reality. Much modern *Self-Help* philosophy is aimed at discovering and developing this empowering sense of autonomy, the convincing evidence of our apparent individuality. And yet, does such an independent Self really exist? And if so, is it as free of others as we are led to believe? It is these often ignored, but vital questions that I will attempt to address throughout the course of this little book.

The *dark-matter* of our being appears to be a mysterious psycho-spiritual substance known as desire; that insatiable energy which drives us towards what we want to possess, or more tellingly, in the direction of who we want to be. The key question though, is whether such desire springs from our autonomous psyche-soul or is it absorbed from a much more subtle, all-encompassing source, the inter-personal *desire-matrix*. In *The Nazarene And The Matrix* I aim to chart this largely hidden ocean of yearning, one on which we attempt to sail our little, illusory barques of individuality.

So, are our desires truly our own? Well, contrary to popular opinion, I believe not. Our inner desire centre is a *receptor* of desire and not its creator. In other words, we are *infected* by the virus-like desire of others, from the cradle to the grave. I'd suggest that each of us receives and subsequently retransmits the desire of others, like some highly efficient server within the network of cyber-space. Sadly, we're not as much of a *one off* as we'd like to believe. Instead, we're part of something much bigger – the all encompassing *desire matrix*.

All desire, by definition, has an object, a something or someone that we wish to acquire. So, with this in mind, let's take a simple example of how desire transference works out in practice: the case of a personal relationship love triangle. A popular, but unattached student has set his hormonal sights on a beautiful girl, one whom he *desires* to date. Unsurprisingly, this young man has himself a group of admirers within the ranks of his male classmates. He's a *model* for them; one whom they subliminally aspire to be. For he has everything that a young man aspires to: good looks, a great sense of humour, a sharp intellect, sporting prowess etc. Now, as one of these male fans begins to observe his laser-like pursuit of the young lady in question, something begins to stir within his own savage breast, viz. *mimetic* or *imitative desire*.

Determined to be like his model, the newly-arrived, secondary suitor begins his *own* campaign of romantic conquest. His first copycat efforts are, of course, inconsequential compared to those of his idealised hero. Yet over time the model admirer begins to realise that he's no longer alone in his romantic endeavours; a rival has now appeared for the beauty's much sought after affections. Retaliatory action must be taken, viz. an intensification of his desire-driven efforts, for after all, she is *meant* to be his. Consequentially, his fan-rival also steps up a gear, thereby initiating a downwardly spiralling, metamorphic process whereby he'll eventually become a *mirror image* of his desire emitting idol. During the course of such a mimetic fascination, the *hero-model* gradually transforms into a *model-obstacle* in the eyes of his previous admirer, viz. one who blocks the progress of *his* amorous goals.

At a critical point in this love-hate desire dance, something dramatically game-changing occurs. Suddenly, the girl is no longer the goal of the young men's mirrored desire. The intensity of their gaze no longer focuses on her or her acceptance of their approaches, but rather on each other. The fight has become everything; its obsessive energy now *possessing* the warring students as they seek to defeat one another in the struggle for victory. The two rivals have become each other's model obstacle, *monstrous doubles* in the devious, yet subliminal, desire battle. A seasoned, neutral observer no longer perceives the clear superiority of one candidate, but concludes that the two, love crazy competitors have inadvertently become clones of one another in the mutual fascination game. The pair can no longer afford to take their psycho-spiritual eyes of one another, for such a demonstration of weakness could spell instantaneous defeat in the vicious desire struggle. Their fight of passion inevitably descends into the depths of relational chaos, where to lose, they mistakenly believe, is to undergo the destruction of their very S*elf*. The bitter consequences of subconscious, mimetic infection have well and truly come to pass, viz. relational breakdown and the threat of potential violence.

We have finally arrived at the tragic scenario of *warring brothers* or *twins*, as depicted in many strands of mythical literature. Seen in the light of mimetic theory, is it any wonder that twins are taboo in many indigenous cultures? The ancestral fathers of ancient history clearly understood the inherent dangers of dynamic mirror images and their potential for endemic, violent contagion.

May I suggest that we all live in the ever-changing, dynamic flux of inter-personal desire transfer. None of us is averse to being hooked by this insidious mechanism of absorbed desire. Our psychological default settings fail to safeguard us from invasive, subliminal infection, indeed they encourage it. Family, friends, work colleagues, faith relationships - all lie within this dysfunctional matrix of pandemic desire. Is it any wonder then, that many of our model-based relationships eventually burst asunder, often with disastrous consequences?

So can we tell if we're presently suffering from a bad case of the *model-obstacles?* Well thankfully linguistics can often come to our rescue. Is anyone presently *getting under your skin* ? Does someone *really get to you*? Is an individual *driving you insane*. If so, then you probably are.

Can we ever be free from the self-destructive nature of our model fascinations? Thankfully, I believe that we can. The liberation of our psyche-soul from the gravitational desire pull of others, shall be an overriding theme of this book.

2

I Wanna Be Like You

We've just seen how the subconscious mimetic process latches onto another's desire, their transmitted yearning for a specific *object*. Our entry into this beguiling, imitative flux eventually leads to a repetitive, tit-for-tat power struggle, one that initially targets the object in question only to be replaced by an obsessive compulsion to achieve a psycho-spiritual victory over our rival or *model obstacle*. This intense fight for *being* quickly becomes a battle of equals, of mutual mirror images or *monstrous doubles*.

During the height of the infamous, Northern Irish Troubles, my late friend Roel Kaptein, a Dutch pastor and mimetic psychologist, was asked, by a high-ranking police officer, how the tragic conflict could be brought to an end.With a slightly mischievous smile, Roel suggested rounding up the Provisional IRA's top leaders for a fancy dress party at police headquarters. The *Provos* would be required to attend in official police uniforms, while the top anti-terrorist officers of Special Branch would don paramilitary attire, including the IRA's signature, black balaclavas.

Needless too say, Roel's distinguished questioner didn't agree to his seemingly bizarre suggestion; political correctness deemed it impossible, even though the insightful adviser had cannily nailed the Irish problem on its head. Both sides' frenzied desire for victory over the other had lost sight of their original object of desire, viz. ownership of the little piece of Earth respectively known as *Ulster* or *The North*. Victory had become their new goal; the perceived power of the *other*, was now the object of desire. Lifting both sets of leaders out of their traditional *roles* by making them dress like their opposing *model obstacles*, would defuse the spiralling mimetic bomb. Twenty five years on, the two warring sides finally put to bed their bitter rivalry after much tragic and totally unnecessary blood-letting. Today, the former Provisional leaders, now reinvented as caring, Armani-suited politicians, share political power with their previous Unionist foes. Roel's little, offbeat role-play has prophetically come to pass.

Of course, some of us choose a desire Model who is way beyond our reach, one totally out of our league. While we may passionately desire to share their *being*, we won't be able to engage them in a close proximity, *monstrous doubles* conflict. Such a Model usually oozes the transcendence of *otherness*, a sublimity that subconsciously hypnotises us into declaring, "I wanna be like *you*". Yet, this desire will always remain unfulfilled, for the Model is so far above us, that we'll never be able to compete as *equals*.

An example of this type of Model selection is the media-induced fame game, as played out by fanatical fans of movie, sports or rock stars. The *celebrity* in question appears to *have* what we *lack;* that missing x-factor which could elevate us to their *godlike* status. Yet, no matter how much money or time we frantically spend in trying to get *into* their world, we repeatedly end up in angst-filled frustration and defeat. Stalkers, the bane of the rich and famous, are also born in this heady cauldron of mimetic desire. The star Model regularly declares, via their well oiled PR machine, a tantalising message: *"Be Like Me!"* And yet paradoxically, through their aloofness and tight security, they forcefully shout, *"Keep Away"*. The infected fan's escalating, but ultimately futile attempts to impress their idol, may eventually drive them to tragic acts of violence. *"Okay, I will replace ......"*, concludes their skewed, addicted logic. Modern mass media continually channels the virus of mimetic desire, one that teasingly promises us a share in its A, B or C list personalities. This barrage of celebrity Models promises much, but inevitably leads us into a confusing psycho-spiritual road block where we're not quite sure who *we* are.

Thankfully, most of us don't play the *out of reach* Model game to such a desperate extent, and yet, we unwittingly participate in lesser, but equally destructive, desires pastimes. By setting our subliminal sights on something or someone nearer to home, we're also consigning ourselves to the downward spiral of recurrent defeat. The endgame is always the same: an ever deepening *depression,* a crippling belief that, *"I'm no good; if only I was like.....".* May I respectfully suggest that much of our personal depression is a consequence of *blocked* mimetic desire, our frenzied, but frustrated attempt to possess the transcendence of *another* whom we ardently admire?

Some of us find ourselves drawn to *high ideal*s, rather than Model personalities. Loyalty, patriotism, morality, love, yes, even *faith* itself can transmit a gravitational desire towards our vulnerable, love-starved psyche. If we could only achieve our metaphysical state of choice, then we will have *won* our battle for being and significance. Amazingly, we can even enter into a misguided rivalry with the Divine itself, one often subtly disguised as the pursuit of holiness, the energetic driving force of much Christian piety. Texts like *"Be ye perfect (mature) as your Heavenly Father is perfect"* have been misinterpreted by somber zealots as proof texts to vindicate their participation in the competitive *holiness game.*

Unfortunately, such a religious mindset is easily manipulated by others, especially those in positions of authority within our particular faith group brand. By channelling and encouraging their desire to be *godly,* they subtly draw their followers into an seemingly noble, mimetic game - one that is bound to fail. For by definition there is only *one* Divine Source, and it lies *way beyond* our ego's futile efforts at imitation. Our strivings to be holy, loving, sacrificial, etc., are in fact telling symptoms of a deeply deceptive mimetic game; one initiated, not in the Divine Heart, but in our desperation to be like the Model par excellence, viz. The Cosmic Parent. May this be the real reason why many regularly *fall away* from such zealous and, to all appearances, admirable religious life? The debilitating depression that constantly shadows our pious efforts eventually takes its tragic toll. Our *skewed desire centre* gives up on Divinity only to find another; a much more attainable Model to emulate and rival.

Can we escape from this psycho-spiritual contagion, the desire-driven life with its enticing but deadly fascinations? How do we detach from our obsessive, vampire-like thirst for the life-force of another? Hopefully we'll find some answers in the next chapter.

3

Copy Cats

When we burst forth into this school-room world of form, we're quickly introduced to our assigned, mimetic teacher, viz. our mother from whom we initially take our imitative cues. She plays the key role in transmitting the postnatal desire field, one in which we find ourselves totally vulnerable to the influence of another. Critically, our very survival depends on quickly coming into harmony with *the way* our mother wishes us to be. It's in these early formative days that numerous pips of parental desire, mainly unconscious, are planted in the deep, receptive recesses of our embryonic psyche; psycho-spiritual seeds that may only come to fruition in later life.

Over time, we're all exposed to the big wide world of people, cultures, institutions, and ideologies, all of which draw us close through the gravitational pull of imitative desire. Their promised pay-off is a strong sense of *identity*, indeed *being*, as long as we remain fertile ground for their psychic propagation. They comprise a swirling sea of desire; one from which we can't fully escape until the day of our last breath.

Like chaotic, fairground bumper cars, we constantly collide with *significant others,* those with attractive desire energies, changing and learning as we go. Shockingly, it's this all-pervasive *desire matrix* that makes us *who we are*. Such interactions may be categorised as *good* or *bad*, depending on the resulting nature of their inter-personal attachments, but more of that later on. The startling revelation is that for each moment of our conscious existence, we appear to be willing victims of *outer mimesis,* that magnetic desire pull emanating from *external significant others*.

But where does that leave our personal sense of *individuality* or *personality*? Well, let's consider these ego perceptions as the results of ongoing mimetic encounter. For example, a mother who obsessively warns her child regarding an external danger will transmit her fear into its open, receptive psyche. This maternal, addictive desire to be constantly heeded, will in time, bear fruit: a permanently deep-seated fear that the child will carry with it, long into adult life. In other words, if we're continually exposed to the emotional transmissions of another, particularly in early childhood, we will eventually internalize these emotions as our own, having them constantly on file, so to speak, for future occasions.

This explains why an individual can be described as, *"just like your mother"*, even though the matriarch in question has long since departed. This internalization of repeated, external interventions on the young psyche produces the desired, or not so desired, result, viz. a *clone* of the original, external transmitter. Our inner tapes of the initial transmission are often triggered in adulthood when encountering situations similar to those of the original. In other words, we begin to imitate our internal psychic self, that *pseudo-personality* planted within by others, during past periods of intensive *external mimesis*.

Without inner mimesis and its looped response, we'd be frantically changing character every second of the day, in a constant state of emotional turmoil, tossed to and fro by every inter-personal desire that came our way. A measure of predictable consistency is gradually added to our psychic mix as we automatically refer to our pre-recorded, internal, instruction manual. As with its external cousin, this inner mimesis can be perceived as *good* or *bad*, depending on the level of freedom and maturity that it produces within the individual.

So life, as we experience it, is a constantly swinging pendulum; one that oscillates between the ever present desire pulls of *outer* and *inner mimesis*. Such a gravitational process can go fairly smoothly or, more rarely, rapidly descend into one of total chaos. All significant re-calibrations of our inner *copy cat* guide only occur when we enter the overwhelming desire field of a newly embraced human transmitter.

In a very real sense we are *all* prisoners of each others' skewed desire fields. Imagining ourselves to be free in our illusory state of autonomy, we can't see the puppet strings that make us dance to the wants and wishes of significant others. It is onto this manipulative, space-time stage that the Nazarene, Yeshua bar Yosef stepped, with His proposed solution.

"Follow me – absorb my desire field and become as I Am -a Clone of Divine Love.

Surely a radical intervention from beyond, the invitation

to freedom from the *"nothing ever changes"* tapes of our internal mimesis. The very essence of *salvation* itself.

4

You, Me And Gravity

I've just outlined how *mimesis,* or unconscious imitation, takes one of two forms, viz. *outer* or *inner.* The former involves the subliminal absorption of another person's desire, while the latter is the process whereby we repeatedly reinforce our existing inner tapes. Coming into contact with a powerful, new desire field, one transmitted by a person, group or ideology, we automatically tweak our internal desire settings and change. Such is the all-pervasive psycho-dynamics of our human condition. External encounter followed by internal assimilation.

So how come we're strongly influenced by certain folk, yet not by others, as we progress through life? The answer lies in the realm of *inter-personal gravitation.* Now, gravitation, the invisible force that keeps our feet firmly on the ground, baffled scientists for centuries until Sir Isaac

Newton, the famous 17th century academic, came up with his Universal Law of Gravitation. During my previous incarnation as a High School Mathematics teacher, I regularly indoctrinated my poor students with this gem from the great professor's genius mind. Anyway, the apple-struck scientist came up with the following formula:

$$F = (Gm_1m_2) / r^2$$

If you hate Math, look away now, but if you stick with it the psycho-spiritual application of Newton's unexpected discovery may just keep you sane. In the above formula F = the gravitational force or pull between two bodies of matter. G = a fixed number, known as the Gravitational constant, m_1 and m_2 = the masses or amount of matter in the respective bodies, whilst r = the physical distance between them.

The physical implications of this Newtonian Law are two-fold. Firstly, the *closer* together two bodies are, the *greater* the gravitational pull between them. Secondly, if one of the masses is extremely large then it will exert an enormous gravitational influence on the smaller, secondary body. For example, the moon is held in Earth's gravitational orbit as a result of Earth's relatively superior mass size. *"All very interesting,"* you may say, *"but how does Sir Isaac's discovery apply to my inter-personal and group relationships?"* Well, let me make a few suggestions.

We're locked into our personal relationships by means of gravitational desire, that transmitted by the *other*. Similarly, we're held fast in our social groups by the collective gravitational desire generated by its members, and in particular, its leaders.

As images of the Divine, each of us transmits a level of mimetic desire, thereby drawing others into our sphere of psycho-spiritual influence. The fact that you're presently reading this chapter would suggest that somehow, through the medium of my writing, something in you has *picked up* or *resonated with* something in me. Perhaps my desire for meaning has locked onto a similar desire for meaning within you. In other words, the transmitted mimetic desire of *others* is constantly drawing us into *our* interests, hobbies, and activities; those *things* on which we spend our time, energy and money. Yet, even more importantly, it draws us into a view of ourselves.

Let's take a simple example of this inter-personal, gravitational pull: a mother and her young infant. A mother clearly has a tremendous desire *mass* in contrast to her child, whose psychic mass is still extremely small. Significantly, both the psychological and physical spaces between them are also minute in the infant's early years. These two telling factors draw the child into an almost total mimesis with their life-moulding mother. A *balanced* mother generally replicates a *balanced* child. On the other hand, a *dysfunctional* mother tragically replicates a mini clone of herself.

A charismatic leader, no matter what his sphere of influence, possesses a heavy desire mass, resulting in an almost irresistible gravitational pull on those of low mass. The rise of Adolf Hitler in a diminished and financially insecure, post-war Germany is a case in point. For some inexplicable reason, the dysfunctional Führer possessed extreme levels of both personal and nationalistic desire. Such was its mimetic dynamic that it pulled a whole nation into his manic, all-conquering ambitions.

A crowd also possesses a large desire mass, due to its internal network of mimetic bonds. It easily pulls an individual into its embodied *oneness* by means of its heightened subliminal transmissions. Anyone who's ever attended a large sports event or rock concert quickly finds themselves momentarily *losing* their individuality, as they join the energised mimetic mass and its promise of collective transcendence.

When we encounter a person or group with a powerful desire transmitter, *individuated freedom* is difficult to maintain. Against our better judgement, we often find ourselves being drawn and moulded into a support act clone of our desire-mass Model. So then, what exactly is freedom? Is it the ability to remain unaffected by an *other*, whether an individual, group, nation, or indeed, an ideology. How can such a Utopian freedom be attained?

Thankfully, Newton's theoretical formula comes to our rescue! If we dwell in close proximity to an individual or group with a strong gravitational mass then it's extremely difficult to maintain our individual sense of freedom. Mathematics would suggest that the only way to diminish the imprisoning pull is to distance oneself from the physical proximity of the transmitter in question. Even a little separation will produce a significantly reduced mimetic force, one granting us a much needed taste of freedom.

Such *distancing* is vital in the tragic world of victim abuse, whether physical, emotional or spiritual. A battered wife is immediately advised to leave the family home and check into a specialised refuge. Why? Well, not only for reasons of physical safety, but also as a first step in breaking free from the hypnotic pull of her dysfunctional spouse. Bullies of all shades have a strong desire pull, one emanating from their hyper-defensive ego, the fragmented psyche formed by early primal wounding.

Returning to Ireland, following my three months detox in distant California, I knew that I couldn't return to the tight-knit Christian sect that I'd spent so many years orbiting. The gravitational desire field of both the group and its charismatic leaders remained a potent force. My newly rediscovered Self identity would have wilted in the intense desire matrix of their hothouse religion. So, for the sake of Self and sanity, I had to pull away. Incidentally, my sense of personal freedom has since further increased after relocating to England, far from my Northern Irish homeland. Escaping from the gravitational pull of Irish culture, with its heady mix of puritanical religion and political tribalism, has proved a real lifesaver.

Finally, here are a few, pertinent questions for us to ponder in our more reflective moments.

Whose desire planet am I presently circling around?

What psycho-spiritual Death Star has locked its tractor beam onto me?

Do I feel like an insignificant, forgotten, little moon, one with no clear direction of my own?

The steps to freedom are simple and within our reach; yet ones that require a certain measure of personal courage. To disengage we must:

Clearly and honestly identify those exerting a great desire mass in our life, those stifling our personal sense of identity.

Place a significant distance, whether psychological, physical or both, between ourself and the desire transmitter in question, even if it signals the end of the pseudo-relationship.

"I need some space" isn't, as is commonly thought, a relational cop-out, but a vital necessity for our continued spiritual, mental and physical well-being. Time to move on perhaps?

5

Cultural Band-Aids

Skewed, mimetic desire lies at the very heart of our human predicament. Drawn into another's gravitational energy field, we unwittingly take the first steps towards contagious rivalry and its eventual fruit, viz. social violence. This deadly desire matrix permanently envelops humankind, resulting in the brutal violence that daily stuns us via our TV news bulletins. Yet, how come our passion crazed species hasn't already decimated itself at some cataclysmic stage in prehistory? Well, ego, the greeter of all our incoming desires, is an expert in the art of survival; ingenious in its evolutionary invention of systems to protect us from individual and communal annihilation. Please let me explain.

As acquisitive desire, rivalry and violence mushroomed within the tribal groupings of early man, a *devilish* thought entered the human mindset for the first time; its flawed logic ran something like this:

"The failings within our community are not the responsibility of the group as a whole, but lie at the feet of a certain individual. Get rid of that individual and our communal problems will go away, at least temporarily."

And so, the *scapegoat victim* was born, that unfortunate individual chosen to be *sacrificed* for the good of all. A designated target of simmering communal violence, the scapegoat's future was not rosy; their *providential* emergence in the midst of contagious rivalry provided a *deserving* victim for the delusional crowd. At best, *the chosen one* was banished from the group and its precious food supply, at worst they'd be granted an instantaneous, one-way ticket to the next life.

Strange as it may seem, the shedding of the hapless victim's blood, or *sacrifice,* proved cathartic for the community at large, having exhausted its deadly desire energy in the frenzied act of murder. A calming, pseudo-peace was restored, at least until a new desire contagion once more drove the community to the brink of annihilation. A new crisis and a new solution, or perhaps more accurately, a new victim.

And so the foundation stone of communal human life, viz. *culture,* was born. A canopy of overarching peace, one paradoxically obtained through so-called acts of *righteous* violence; the immediate influx of restored calm only *confirming* the apparent guilt of the helpless victim in the eyes of all.

Now, as culture and its scapegoat mechanism evolved, the following phenomena gradually emerged:

Ritual

Ritual is the communal re-enactment of a sacrificial event. In such an event, the victim or victimized group is initially the target of dark humour or comedy, as in Nazi Germany's 1930s' depiction of the Jews. Next, the scapegoating focus is finely sharpened. The victim is selected for *death*, the transference of the community's flaws having already taken place. This is the stage of *tragedy,* one which permeates the works of all great literature. The third stage in the sacrificial drama is the uninhibited exhibition of communal joy in expressive music and dance; the celebration that the community has *put things to right,* often with the whole-hearted support of their transcendent god.

Myths

Myths are simply stories told by the community after their expulsion of the scapegoat; foundation tales to reinforce the beneficial effects of the *sacrifice*. Passed down from one generation to another, they attempt to explain why *we* are the way we are. In such folklore, the community is always *right* and the victim always *wrong*. In other words, myths hide the ever-present scapegoat mechanism, thus maintaining a level of *self-righteous* continuity for *our people*.

Myths, in turn, give birth to *morality,* our ethical system of designating the *good* and the *bad*. No one lies outside the sphere of our moral judgements. Those whom we encounter are both quickly and easily judged on the basis of our communal or individual myths. The *other* is now a member of *our* community, or more disturbingly, a potential *scapegoat*. All success within a moralising culture is at the cost of a scapegoat. *"I've made it, and you haven't."* Such is the basis for our one-*upmanship,* that psycho-spiritual power game played within our cultural strata of choice.

Each of us has our own particular *myth* narrative to tell;

a story for ourselves and others. It's our way of maintaining our sanity in an ever-changing world of relational conflict. The alternative is to risk identifying ourselves as a scapegoat, with all the deadly consequences that would surely follow. No, none of us want to be *done-away with*, and so we continue to play our mythical morality tapes, thereby reassuring both ourselves and others that we're part of the *moral majority*.

Law

Law evolved as a means of keeping a lid on the bubbling cauldron of mimetic desire. It achieves this by establishing a *spatial structure* within human society. We each take *our place* under law, accepting that our desires are subject to its predetermined judgements. When the rule of law breaks down, imitative desire becomes a rampant plague, one resulting in the spiralling violence of mob rule. Hence the *founding murder* principle is once more released into the heart of community. Simply put, law is the band-aid of society. A temporary, but ultimately unsuccessful attempt to solve the skewed desire predicament of societal affairs.

Structure

Structure is a spatial attempt to stop the spread of mimetic desire. A structureless society will be one in which everyone believes they have the right to rival, having all that others have, whether materially, status wise or even metaphysically. However, contrary to popular opinion, such a level playing field doesn't provide the utopian solution for each of us to be as we desire. Rather, it only releases a hyper-acquisitive craving to be like *everyone else* within the community. Ultimately, such an egalitarian viewpoint only stokes the free market fire of desire, an advertiser's commercial heaven. It tends to underestimate the power of mimetic contagion which is *never* satisfied with being like a *limited* number of others. Our psyche's skewed desire centre is unstoppable in its never-ending crusade to be like *everyone*, as it frantically searches for its misplaced identity.

In times past, *structure* has kept many under the authoritarian cosh. It has been, and indeed still is, used as a devious tool of suppression and control. The use of structure to enhance the *power* of the ruling classes, has often proved to be a crude tool in keeping desire at bay. Yet, structural desire boundaries are culture's traditional means of avoiding imitative contagion. Within a global society where *traditional differences* are rapidly disappearing, mimetic desire, as transmitted by mass and social media, has opened up a new can of rivalry worms, ones well-nigh impossible to contain.

As the old, cultural mechanisms creak with fragility in the face of this global onslaught of transmitted desire, where are we to turn for answers to the ever-increasing levels of violence and blood letting? Are we on the brink of a totally unexpected maturation of humankind, or a new form of totalitarianism, the dreaded One World Order of the ever-growing list of conspiracy theorists? Or is there an alternative solution to our 21st century desire epidemic? Well, why don't we ask a scapegoat? In fact, why not ask the scapegoat of all scapegoats, the Nazarene, Yeshua, bar Yosef, more commonly known as *the Christ*.

6

Religion

We've just concluded that human *culture* is constructed with the building blocks of ritual, myths, laws and structures; those safety mechanisms designed by mankind to redirect the destructive energy of mimetic desire and its violent expression into less spreadable forms. It's deeply shocking to discover that culture, in all its revered, multifarious manifestations, has its origins in the mob violence of early human society. Simply put, culture is mankind's attempt at *capping,* or *keeping a lid on,* a desire explosion and its resulting violent shrapnel. How does it do this? Well, simply through the selection of a *scapegoat,* a victimized individual or group, one mistakenly judged to be responsible for the ingrained flaws of whole community. I shall now attempt to look behind the respectable mask of religion, by exploring its hidden association with such a scapegoat mechanism. First let me make a bold and perhaps somewhat provocative statement. *Culture and religion are identical.*

Matrix Messiah

Now culture, with all its inherent self-importance, would certainly disavow this seemingly preposterous association. For its part, religion, oblivious to its own particular brand of self-righteousness, would also brush aside such a blasphemous thought. Yet both religion and culture consist of the same four safety mechanisms adopted to channel desire and restrict violence, viz. ritual, myth, law and structure. Therefore, may I boldly suggest that all religion is cultural, and all culture inherently religious. Only differing linguistic terminologies, those assigned to their shared mechanisms, appear to differentiate them in the eyes of a somewhat gullible mankind.

Religion always sets up camp in the realm of the *scapegoaters*, viz. the community that acts as judge and jury in the never-ending morality game; that ego-driven pastime, played in response to internal desire conflicts. On the other hand, *faith,* or perhaps more accurately *trust,* is the psycho-spiritual home of the *scapegoats,* those unfortunate victims upon whom communal blame has unjustly fallen, often with deeply tragic consequences. Violence is the fertile seed bed in which religion and all its related manifestations quickly take root. I'd better explain.

When violence raised its ugly head within early tribal

societies, an *other* or *scapegoat* was haphazardly selected to act as a human lightning conductor; one to absorb the murderous overflow of the rising tide of discord. The group's justificatory mantra quickly evolved as: *"Better that one die, than our community destroy itself."* By means of their death, the unfortunate victim, the designated *devil in the midst*, appeared to restore a cathartic peace to the frenzied mob whose blood lust had just been satisfied. The community's skewed reasoning continued to salve its reflex conscience with the following religious theory: "This *transcendent* peace that we're now experiencing can only mean one thing: an overseeing god is pleased with our violent undertaking, our approved, and thereby *righteous*, act of murder." Thus the *sacred*, with its underlying desire-birthed dynamic was born.

Where religion prevails, violence, whether physical or emotional, will be close at hand, waiting to offer its services in defence of the group myth. When violence rears its ugly head, ancient, religious memories of blood atonement stir deep within our primal subconscious. Even the nightly habit of watching the TV news becomes a religious ritual, one adorned with our self-righteous judgements of *who's to blame*.

This fascination with violence always involves our base religious instincts, evidenced by our automatic search for a victim to blame. The alternative, a careful examination of our own internal desire conflicts, is too painful for our wounded psyche to contemplate. Searching out potential victims via the mass media or within our close-knit circles, we're acting out of our own myth narrative: that *fantastical* story which constantly reassures us that we won't be the next scapegoat. This fear of being the *burnt offering* to come, is the essence of all religious thought and practice. The distant, transcendent god has *laws* that must be adhered too at all costs. To break them is to incur a death sentence, either figuratively or literally: the scapegoat selection that none of us yearn for.

Unsurprisingly, no matter what our spiritual paradigm, none of us like to be considered religious, and yet, every time we entertain violent thoughts we're being drawn into the religious contagion that encircles us. When we defend our *beliefs* against those of the *"devil in our midst"*, we're playing our part, albeit unknowingly, in the raging, mimetic mob. By wearing the robes of self-righteousness, those smeared in the blood of another, we're playing our hypocritical role in the deeply religious, yet tragic drama.

Some of us believe that by buying into a new brand of religious belief, all shall be well. Yet, by scapegoating our old religious system, we only repeat the blame games of bygone days We can't detach from our *moral murderer* within, no matter how *loving* our new, spiritual world view. The enthusiastic, mind, body, spirit devotee can be as religious as the fundamentalist, monotheistic believer. The renowned, atheistic author can be participating in the ritualistic *god game* alongside the backwoods, hellfire preacher.

As 21st century, Western society, with its creaking rituals, myths, laws and structures, begins to implode, religion with its black and white, dualistic certainties appears to be heading for the rocks. Only in the emerging Third World do multitudes of souls still feverishly climb into the utopian lifeboat of fundamentalist promises. So, can the execution of Yeshua bar Yosef, the Nazarene Prophet shed any light on our current religio-cultural predicament? Can it be interpreted without viewing it through the *religious* lens of much traditional Christian theology, without labelling the god of the Galilean as a violent judge, one requiring the blood sacrifice of His cherished Son? I suspect that the truth is more shocking than we've been led to believe by two thousand years of religious desire capping. But more of that in the next chapter

7

I Don't Like To Judge, But......

Many who follow the religious or spiritual path, are often labelled *hypocrites* by those outside their particular group or belief system. Yet, what exactly is hypocrisy and is it legitimate to brand others as such? Well, hypocrisy is most commonly defined as: *"the practice of claiming to have moral standards or beliefs to which one's own behaviour does not conform."* In other words, *pretence*.

Nevertheless, surely this somewhat painful definition requires further clarification. If I pretend to be something that I'm consciously not, then I'm not a hypocrite, but rather a *deceiver*. The insidious essence of hypocrisy is that it is totally *unrecognised* by the hypocrite them-self; it's a deep stream of inconsistency that bypasses the host's conscious mind. The hypocrite is totally unaware that they are one! Hypocrisy is a *hidden* enemy, one that lurks in the dark recesses of our psycho-spiritual makeup.

As we live within culture and its twin associate, the realm of religion, we daily inhale the air of hypocrisy. The scapegoating mechanism, of which we all partake, is the communal outworking of such hypocrisy. By participating in the ritual condemnation of others, we genuinely believe ourselves to be *right* and the other party *wrong*. The possibility that *we* could be wrong, and hence someone else's scapegoat, is too painful for us to contemplate; the thought just doesn't enter our heads.

Our everyday lives are oiled by this veiled hypocrisy; one that temporarily enables us to feel good about ourselves, whilst looking down our noses and psychically stoning the maligned *other*. Morality, in all its various forms, provides a self-righteous veneer of respectability to our condemnation of the *goat* or *devil-god* in our midst, the one judged responsible for all our ills. If only *they* were driven out, excluded from our personal or communal lives, then all would be well. Little do we realise that their apparent *sins* reside deep within our *own* wounded psyche; only too ready to reveal their fragmented hand when a suitable opportunity arises. *"There, but for the grace of God go I, and all that!"*

Surprisingly though, wakening up to the truth of the scapegoat mechanism and its clandestine cloak of hypocrisy, doesn't guarantee our freedom from its *devilish* power. Recognising hypocrisy may just make us even bigger hypocrites. The knowledge of how society and individuals operate can become a new, more powerful weapon in our ostracising, ritual power-plays. Our radical, new insight may attempt to place us *above* the masses and their inherent violence; thereby reinforcing our ego's sense of separation from the scapegoats, our broken fellow-man. In reality, we're all both scapegoaters and scapegoats, depending on our particular social milieu. Our limpet-like, hypocrisy is a tricky dysfunction to shift in our struggle for psycho-spiritual freedom. Indeed, even the very desire for freedom, may prove to be just another crafty ploy for enthroning us as god-like scapegoaters.

So, who can deliver us from this insidious state of affairs? Well, I believe that Yeshua bar Yosef, the embodiment of our non-rivalling, *Source Transcendence,* is the only one qualified to shine the spotlight on our hidden hypocrisy, without the kick-back threat of infection. Now, the Galilean prophet certainly didn't hold back in his scalpel-like diagnosis of hypocrisy within the prevailing

Pharisaic mindset of His day. Yet, may this apparent act of *judgement* not be reinterpreted as the Nazarene's most shocking act of *supreme love*. A brave deed, that surely sealed his fate in the religio-political bull ring of first century Palestine. Living outside the gravitational field of mimetic rivalry, uniquely qualified the Nazarene to shine Divine Light into the whitewashed dark recesses of our human hypocrisy.

So where does all this leave us? Well, whether we like it or not, we *are* all hypocrites; yet, hypocrites who are welcomed back into the arms of Divine Love. Secular or religious – it doesn't matter, for we all have the genes of hypocrisy swirling around in our defence-driven egos; that gnawing fear of being scapegoated by those close to us, our dreaded transformation into the *devil-god* of religion.

Thankfully, Divine Love's embrace doesn't depend upon our position in the scapegoater rankings. Fully aware that we play the alternating roles of scapegoater and scapegoat, *Source Presence* still welcomes us into its all consuming Union, that place of ultimate security where hypocrisy withers and dies.

To walk in the *Spirit Breath* of Divine Love is the *only* effective antidote to the rampant hypocrisy and insidious judgements that plague our human hearts. Living in our desire-driven, dysfunctional culture, with its accompanying, big topped, scapegoating circus, is an experience that will eventually drive us back into the arms of Innocence. Paradise regained.

8

Feelings

In the Jewish model of spirituality, human feelings originated in the gut or abdomen, the perceived residence of Divine Spirit. Yeshua bar Yosef, the Galilean prophet, publicly proclaimed that those who would believe into, or come into mimesis with, Him, would experience a spiritual energy, (Living Water) flowing from their inner cavity or belly. *"Metaphorical nonsense,"* you might say, and yet, modern scientific research is discovering that we do possess a highly developed *sensory* network within the human stomach, one just as powerful as that found in the brain. When we're bowled over by a beautiful sunset, or a majestic forest of Giant Redwoods, we are emoting as a result of a subliminal encounter with Divine Other, via our *psycho-spiritual gut*. Most of the time though, we operate out of an entirely different place, as we're constantly manipulated by the desire bombardment of the modern world. What we commonly describe as *emotions,* are usually no more than the knocks that come our way in the rivalry pastime of bumper car relationships.

For Yeshua however, *feelings* were birthed out of His well developed sense of security and non-rivalry with Divine Love, the One intimately referred to by Him as *Abba Alaha*. All His other relationships, even those with His adversarial religious opponents, must be understood in the context of His unique, relational freedom and detachment.

By contrast, our experience of what we commonly term feelings, is always linked to an *other*. Our *fragmented psyche-soul,* or *ego,* always transmits feelings as messages of defeat or victory in our subliminal power struggles with those around us. Feelings are *never* just *personal,* but subtly connected to the complex matrix of humanity, that swirling ocean in which we find ourselves immersed. As we encounter a new individual, we automatically slot into an unconscious imitation of them, whether we like to acknowledge it or not. Their *mimetic,* gravitational pull will often trigger the replay of our old *feeling* tapes, ones recorded during previous desire encounters. It takes time, and lots of it, for us to finally realise that our feelings are birthed in the womb of inter-personal relationships.

In this mimetic model of modern feelings, we ride an ego-fuelled roller coaster with its alternating thrills of good and bad feelings, all transpiring on the track of relational rivalry. When a feeling suddenly appears out of nowhere, a relationship, whether past or present, will always lie behind it.

So let's examine some of our most common *feelings*, as interpreted within the context of relational power plays. Of course, feelings are extremely complex little phenomena, yet this simple, little diagnosis may help us begin to unravel their internal history.

Elation & Depression

Elation is birthed by victory in the scapegoating game; a somewhat euphoric sense of being *one-up* on the other. *Losing* a relational power play always results in *depression*. Such a feeling of downheartedness almost always stems from a stubborn, *Model Obstacle* relationship, one that we can't get past. Both feelings are usually associated with someone to whom we are very attached, e.g. controlling family relationships.

Masochism

Strange as it may seem, we can *enjoy* permanently losing to our *Model Obstacle*. Our recurring defeats paradoxically reinforce our warped view of them as a *god*, one that it is our perverted pleasure to serve. We worship the other's *sadism* from our highly valued position of victimhood.

Fear and Anger

Fear flows from the all too real possibility of becoming the next scapegoat, the one to be *ostracised* or, to put it more bluntly, *got rid of*. It always comprises the prospect of losing something, particularly our sense of Self. Often, we can be paralysed by the apparent strength and overwhelming power of the *other*. Anger is our resulting attempt to *expel* or *drive out* the other within us; to finally rid ourselves of their all-controlling, suffocating presence within our sacred space.

Tears and Laughter

Laughter is our reflex attempt to *shake off* the threat posed by the *other;* our effort to see them as smaller than they first appear to our fearful psyche. Stand up comedians exercise great mimetic power in elevating their audiences to the role of communal scapegoaters. Such strength in numbers always empowers us to look down our noses at our potential scapegoaters. *Tears,* on the other hand, are our attempt at throwing a curve ball at an approaching rival. The closer they are *to us,* or perhaps more accurately, *into us,* the more likely we are to detonate this explosive weapon of mass destruction in our highly-charged power game. Crying is usually our last-ditch attempt at removing the *other* from our psychic space.

Enthusiasm

A deeply religious word, enthusiasm suggests that we've been taken over or possessed by a god-like *other*. We have been granted a divine power supply, one to aid us in the battle with our rival. Enthusiasm is a high level weapon, one that attempts to permanently get rid of our adversarial *devil-god* or *Model Obstacle*.

Sexuality

Much modern sexuality has morphed into a subtle power game. To take over or dominate another's body is the ultimate form of one-*upmanship.* This sense of *possession by* or *invasion of* another can become an enticing power supply in our inter-personal ego wars.

Ideals

When ideals or ultimate goals reside within our psyche, we're often launched on a Utopian journey, one that's bound to end in tears. As we endeavour to live up to our *Model ideal,* it quickly becomes an obstacle as we repetitively fail in our vain attempts to achieve it. This Model mindset morphs into our own personal prison, one that condemns us to forever play the role of loser scapegoat in our frenzied, spiritual quest.

Fascination

Fascination is one of the most powerful and potentially dangerous feelings that we can encounter. It allows the *other* to take up residence within all the rooms of our personal psychic space. Unlike other feelings, it stakes its domineering claim in every sub-personality of our inner life. Embracing this exciting, but ultimately dangerous guest, we push aside all the other possibilities for our life, being totally *sold out* to this person or ideal. Riding our fascination wave of choice can be extremely exhilarating, but once we fall off we immediately hit the depths of dark despair. Indeed, many violent crimes of passion often occur during this angst-ridden period of utter disillusionment.

So how are we to detach from these pseudo-feelings, those that initially promise much only to finally imprison us? May I suggest that withdrawal from the vicious loop of imitative desire is the only way out. Yet, who's genuinely qualified to open the door of our mimetic jail? Well, I believe it to be Yeshua bar Yosef, the Nazarene prophet-teacher who lives in non-rivalling mimesis with Divine Source. He is the One to lead us into experiential freedom, a new way of life far from the ups and downs of emotional captivity.

"Come, follow Me. Enter into my liberating, mimetic connection with Divine Love."

9

New World Waiting

Bursting onto the religious scene of his day, Yeshua bar Yosef immediately presented a shocking challenge to his listeners. He urged them to step *out* of the world of *mimetic or imitative* conflict and into the realm of detached peace, commonly referred to as *the Kingdom of God*. Interestingly, the Aramaic word *malkutha,* the one chosen by the Nazarene to describe this spiritual realm, is a feminine noun, perhaps better translated *Queendom* but that's another theological twist for another time.

To wake up and discover that we're being offered an altogether *different kind* of Life by Divine Source, is a bit of a seismic shock to our psycho-spiritual wiring. Over the years we become accustomed to our relentless *ego wars,* those ups and downs of *desire struggle* engaged in by our sub-personalities. *"You win some, you lose some,"* becomes our mantra of compromise, as we steadily march towards the grave. Yet, all around us, social structures, which have previously limited our mimetic battles, are beginning to crumble. Egalitarianism has freed many from abusive, authoritarian control, but has inadvertently birthed a new problem, viz. *unleashed, widespread desire.* In other words, we all desire to have what everyone else appears to have or desire. Even more insidiously, we crave to *be* whom others appear to be. The gloves are finally off in our dark desire wars. *"I want to be famous, like you,"* the underlying motivation of TV Reality Show participants, has become the clarion call for our ever shrinking 21st century, global village.

In the midst of such chaos, our metaphysical desire for peace grows stronger by the day. Attempting to recommission the old sacrificial systems, we raise our level of violence against *the other* in order to release the *pseudo-transcendent peace* that appears to flow from their bloody demise. The modern double-act of *terrorism* and *counterterrorism* is a lost and confused community's attempt to raise the stakes in its desire for victorious peace, one that is ultimately destined to fail.

As we scramble around looking for *someone to be*, the

Nazarene graciously steps in, confidently inviting us to follow Him. Yet, why *should* we follow Him or His radical teachings? His followers appear to be just as screwed up and involved in mimetic rivalry games as the rest of us! Well, Yeshua calls us back to the Innocence of Eden, the mythic Garden nursery of our beginnings; the home of serenity and non rivalry where all flows from, and toward, Divine Source. The sheer impossibility of rivalling the Divine in this New World, allows the peace that we so yearn for, to rush into our psycho-spiritual core, like fresh, cool air into panting lungs.

Within this Queendom, realigned desire structures provide the possibility of an authentic, transcendent peace, one that is truly *Other* in nature. Paradoxically, yielding to Divine Love brings a new-found freedom, one impossible to experience in the ego-channelled world of desire. The primal desire to be an image of Divine Love itself, rather than the cloned image of an *other*, finds its fulfilment as we follow the Galilean in his mimetic role as incarnated Son. This Prototype of Divine progeny beckons us on as we begin to discover our own Divine lineage, our original, mimetic relationship with the Source of Divine Love. Growing in the awareness of our Divine heredity, we

Matrix Messiah

become the very extension of a Presence that desires to fill all in all. Now, that's what I call a New World worth getting into!

10

The Man From Beyond

We've just seen how Yeshua bar Yosef came to announce the *Queendom of God,* that inner realm lying beyond the dysfunctional reach of our skewed, human desire. Yet, what qualified the Galilean rabbi to proclaim the imminent arrival of this potential, seismic shift in mankind's psycho-spiritual alignment? Well, let's have a look at some of the Nazarene's unique qualities, those that hint at His mysterious *Otherness.*

Of course, Yeshua was fully human; there can be no doubt about that. The early, gnostic tendency to perceive him as a visiting spirit, one free of human limitations is deeply appealing, yet not really plausible. No, this radical prophet was definitely flesh and blood like us, even if the embryonic rumours of His mysterious conception might have suggested otherwise. Nevertheless, the carpenter turned itinerant rabbi was different, for He was a man who lived outside the gravitational matrix of mimetic desire. In other words, he constantly operated out of His spiritual gut, rather than the transmitted desires of others.

Yeshua's desert encounter with the adversarial *Satan*, the very personification of desire rivalry, reveals the liberating source of his psycho-spiritual life. The desire pull of the tempting *other* couldn't latch onto the detached psyche-soul of the tired and hungry Galilean. His mimetic alignment proved to be with the Divine Will alone. Hence, His unique ability to relate to those around him out of a place of inner freedom. The mythical Garden of Eden encounter had been re-enacted, though this time around, the *Second Adam's* psycho-spiritual desire centre remained totally focused on the *One* from whom he'd come. Instead, it was the Satan of skewed, imitative desire who was expelled, rather than the Divine prototype. The Nazarene remained untainted and ready for action, in the desert landscape of the post-Edenic, human condition.

Yeshua also claimed to do only what he saw Divine Source doing; a transcendent, imitation of the highest order. In listening and responding to the revelatory whispers of Divine Will, the Nazarene acted as an authentic *Son of God*, an exact image of the Divine Parent. Unlike the rest of mankind, those of us trapped in the endless cycle of external and internal mimetic rivalry, Yeshua was somehow able to live within the desire matrix without being infected. Detached, yet deeply compassionate, the prophet-teacher reflected the very nature of Divine Love itself.

Our somewhat warped perception of the Transcendent Other, is constantly being sculpted by the sand-storm of desire that surrounds us . Our *God* is often the god of the scapegoater, that all-powerful ally who fights along side us in our inter-personal disputes. Yeshua, on the other hand, radically proposes that by observing Him, we'll discover the essential nature of Divine Source. *"He who has seen me, has seen the Father."*

In his dance of mimetic freedom, the Galilean prophet rises far above the devil-gods of our religious paradigms. We can no longer be spun the lie that *God* authorises our scapegoating of others in the wildfires of human conflict. Yeshua well and truly nails the big lie of religion for all time, by revealing Divine Love as the god of the *scapegoats* rather than the sponsor of the *scapegoaters.* No longer can violence hide behind the masks of political and religious orthodoxy. No longer can it be justified as the righteous Will of the Cosmic Parent on High.

Unaffected by the lure of the desire matrix, Yeshua uniquely perceived the human condition; the universality of imitative violence, a violence often decked out in the guise of moral outrage. His understanding of those with whom he associated was spot on. Knowing what made them tick, allowed Him to remain free of personal rivalries. The Nazarene prophet perceived their subliminal psycho-spiritual chains, as only the Divine could. By drawing them into His own desire field, sickness and mental illness fell away, no longer the attached by-products of *Model-Obstacle* or *Monstrous Double* relationships. Mimetic alignment with the Divine, as modelled by the Galilean, released religious and non-religious alike from the painful consequences of skewed desire.

Yeshua bar Yosef was the harbinger of a new realm; a place free from tit-for-tat reprisals, both personal and collective; a world of realigned connection to the One from whom all come and all will return. Of course, many spiritual teachers within Judaism and beyond had caught glimpses of such a world in times past, yet in the life of the Nazarene, the Queendom was no longer an unobtainable pipe dream but a present face to face reality. A Divine breakthrough, though one that would surely end in tears

11

Crossed Out

An individual operating outside the field of mimetic desire, one fully tuned into the Divine Will, is a dangerous maverick in the world of men. And so it proved in the case of Yeshua bar Yosef. With His radical teaching and proclamation of a new Queendom, the itinerant prophet wasn't going to be awarded a place on the popularity podium by the religio-political rulers of his day. Something had to give! Setting off along the fateful Jerusalem road, the Nazarene fully realised the tragic outcome that awaited him in the courts of men.

When experiencing internal pressures, human society always reverts to its traditional, tried and trusted method of letting off steam. The scapegoat mechanism quickly gets rid of any disturbing grit that threatens to change its autocratic, oyster-like world. And so it was with the Galilean. The political, Roman establishment, with all its centuries of conquest and subjugation, hadn't got to where it was by letting free thinkers have their way. Similarly, institutional Judaism had maintained its tight hold on the Hebrew people by violently gagging their reformist prophets, those doing their thing outside the existing sacred authority structures. Indeed, most of Yeshua's prophetic predecessors had met an extremely sticky, missional end.

A community that feels threatened, always strikes back. The fear of revolt and rapid military reprisals maintained an uneasy alliance between Rome and the Jerusalem establishment; one whose aim was to *get rid* of Yeshua and his outspoken exposés for good. Once designated as scapegoat, the Nazarene faced the anger of the Jerusalem crowd, those who'd backed Him only days before. By coming into mimetic alignment with the perceived wisdom of their elders, their cheers of support and adulation had rapidly morphed into the bloodthirsty cries of the mob. Yet, it came as no surprise to their Galilean victim. Hadn't He exposed the hidden violence of the human ego in much of His teaching? A fractured psyche, one driven by imitative desire, would always strike out when its all important goals were blocked.

In other words, Yeshua had become a *stumbling block* or *scandalon* (Greek) for his opponents, one around whom their raging desire couldn't pass. By being in mimetic harmony with Divine Love, he'd challenged and exposed the hidden drivers of a dysfunctional society and its conventional wisdom. In the normal course of human affairs, a targeted victim would have retaliated by striking back at his enemies, thus setting up a spiralling partnership of M*onstrous* or W*arring Doubles*. Yet, the Nazarene refused to flee Jerusalem or fight back. Instead, He chose to submit to the worst that mob displeasure and establishment violence could throw at him in the none too convincing guise of law and order.

So what did Yeshua, expect from his violent death? Did He suffer from a somewhat masochistic death wish. Was He so disillusioned with his rejection of His message, that he no longer cared? I reckon neither. For something deep within the Nazarene assured Him that He'd been born for such an apparently tragic scenario. He was destined to demonstrate to humanity the authentic nature of Divinity; to put an end to the lie that the God of Israel and violence were cosy bedfellows. By allowing Himself to become the archetypal Innocent Victim, he revealed the inherent hypocrisy of all political and religious power; the societal lie that aligns law and justice with the Source of All. The holy man's hanging, broken body would reveal the shocking *non-violence* of Divine Love; its overwhelming determination not to enter into rivalry with its created Sonship, no matter what the cost.

Something very primal and earth shattering was taking place as the dying Galilean cried out, *"It is finished."* Something much more dangerous than the standard Christian interpretation of payment for sin. Instead, Yeshua bar Yosef, was lifting the lid off the scapegoat mechanism lamp, thereby expelling the genie of violence that loves to lurk within the dark restrictive confines of both religion and culture. No longer could Divinity be accused of siding with the scapegoaters; the omniscient One signed up to authorise the targeting of guilty victims. No, Divine Love had courageously allowed its true colours to be nailed to a bloodied mast, one that doubled-up as a Roman executional device. The *so-called* Cosmic Judge had dramatically revealed Himself as the brutalised Victim of his own Creation. A God whose omnipotence paradoxically lay in the depths of his utter vulnerability.

Yet, how do we know that the Nazarene wasn't just

another failed, deluded, Messianic reformer, one ultimately deserving of His barbaric, but not totally unexpected, end? Well, I'll attempt to answer that most critical question in the next chapter.

12

You Can't Keep A Good Man Down

Something quite unique was playing out on the stage of world history when Yeshua bar Yosef, the itinerant, Nazarene prophet, was expeditiously done away with by the religio-political powers of his day. In the years that followed, many of His followers interpreted this death as a *payment for mankind's sin,* heavily influenced by the traditional, blood atonement rituals of the *Jewish Temple Cult.* According to this particular exegesis, Yeshua's substitutionary death removed the gulf of debt owed to Source Divinity, thereby allowing Spirit Breath to once more reside with mankind. Yet, during His three years on the public stage, Yeshua regularly demonstrated the fallacy of such a theory. His inclusive interactions with those deemed *sinners* by the *self-righteous* of His day, shattered the illusory lie of separation. By definition, the Divine

Nature never changes, so why the sudden request for a blood payment to re-establish relationships with dysfunctional man? No, ego, our wounded psyche-soul is the only exiling judge on the religious block; one paradoxically waiting for an Atonement that it strives to make sure, never happens.

Divine Love's *at-one-ment* began well outside the restrictions of linearly perceived space-time, and as such, is an *always* fact. Source doesn't flick its acceptance of us, off and on, like some transcendent light switch. No, what happened in that insignificant, far-flung outpost of the Roman Empire was much more earth shattering, viz. a bloody, barbaric demonstration of the Innocence of Divine Love and its refusal to join our scapegoating games, those played so viciously by its wounded children. For the first time in human history, a State sponsored execution doubled as a Divine drama, a murder mystery that revealed a shocking truth, viz. there isn't, and never has been, a barrier between God and man, as seen from the Divine perspective. Guilt and blame are *ego's* tools, those honed to keep alive the illusion of separation. The Nazarene, with all his radical talk of a welcoming Divinity, had to be silenced by the powers that be. Bad for religion, bad for politics, and bad for their joint monopoly of human culture, the Galilean's revolutionary message had to be stopped, and no better way to do it than the ruthlessly efficient, Roman way.

So wasn't Yeshua just another well intentioned, but deeply deluded, holy man, one who'd spiritual ambitions way above His earthly station? Hadn't the guardians of human society, well and truly demonstrated that the bloody sacrifice of a scapegoat victim is always the final word? Isn't mankind trapped in an unacknowledged prison of mimetic desire, with no *Queendom of God* to provide a liberating alternative? Wasn't the most talked about death in human history no more than the tragic, early exit of a utopian visionary? I believe not.

Somewhat bizarrely, the Nazarene's closest associates claimed that they'd seen Him alive after his execution and entombment, albeit in a somewhat *different* bodily form. Quantum-like, the Nazarene now that appeared to walk through locked, wooden doors and teleport Himself around at will; not as a spirit, as in previous appearances of the dead, but in some rearranged, physical configuration, one without the normal restrictions of matter.

Of course, many books have already been written by scholars on both sides of the religious fence, regarding this historical claim of bodily resurrection. So, my intention here isn't to enter into the combative world of metaphysical ping pong regarding the claims of the early Yeshua movement. Rather, I wish to interpret such claims as a sign of Divine *validation*. If, as Yeshua had suggested, Divine Source is the god of the *scapegoats,* then what better way to demonstrate the fact than by raising the *supreme scapegoat* from the insidious jaws of death and decay?

It's interesting to note that the scriptural, Greek phrase translated as *"raised from the dead",* suggests a rousing or awakening of the psyche-soul from Hades, the traditional resting place of the dead. This unique reunion of the Galilean's psyche, reconstituted body and spirit essence confirmed that he'd been right all along. The return of the Nazarene from beyond the borders of death, was the authenticating stamp of Divine approval for the One who claimed Union with Divine Source.

In the case of previous spiritual teachers, both Jewish and non-Jewish, the Divine Parent hadn't intervened after their departure from this vale of tears. Yet, catching both grieving followers and smug authorities totally off guard, the dynamic power of Sacred Unity burst the executed prophet back onto the metaphysical stage. An earth shattering act that finally revealed the authentic nature of Divine Love, the One we commonly call God. So how come sacrificial religion and its political bedfellows have made a resounding comeback following such a Divinely orchestrated game-changer? Well, I'll attempt to answer that most puzzling of questions in the next chapter.

13

The Empire Strikes Back

In the previous chapter I suggested that Yeshua bar Yosef, the executed, Galilean preacher-prophet, received an earth-shattering endorsement from Divine Source, by means of a previously unheard of *rousing* from the realm of the dead. Body, (a quantum-like version), soul, (psyche-personality), and spirit, (Divine essence), all appear to have reunited in the risen rabbi. The teasingly playful appearances of this New Man, as narrated in the New Testament Gospels, give us telling glimpses of the Divine Queendom and its liberating nature. Thankfully, the four dimensions of space-time don't appear to apply to this mysterious realm, one where Divine Love consumes All in its Dance of Delivering Delight. Skewed desire no longer appears to have anything in which to embed itself, nothing within to parasitically latch onto. In this liberating sphere, realigned desire flows once more between God and Man.

Outside the somewhat constricting arena of space-time all things are now possible for the risen Master.

Yet, where does all that leave us? Why is our post-resurrection world still in a mess, some two millennia after this supposedly earth-shattering event? Where exactly *is* this utopian realm of Divine rule and why is it only visible to the ego-free, awakened eye? All vital questions that I will now attempt to address.

The fledgling Yeshua movement was birthed and totally energized by the unexpected resurrection and subsequent appearances of their previously deceased Teacher-Friend. Previously fearful and in hiding, the Nazarene's followers suddenly burst forth to proclaim a radical new possibility to the religio-political society of their day. Miraculous signs of the transcendent Queendom broke through the restrictions of space-time, to reveal the restorative nature of the Divine realm. In the years that followed, the evolving Yeshua movement continued on a Spirit-fuelled roll; one that began to threaten the existing cultural order, the traditional bastion of the ancient scapegoat mechanism.

Such an established system, one that had controlled human society since skewed desire did its thing in *The Garden*, wasn't going to simply lie back and surrender, like some subservient puppy waiting for a Divine tummy tickle. No, this mechanistic violence that Yeshua had publicly confronted and exposed in his brutal death, wasn't known as *"The Adversary"* or *"The Satan"* for nothing. It had real teeth and it certainly wasn't afraid to use them. The Nazarene's journey into, and awakening from, Death had exposed the previously hidden, sacred scapegoating, once and for all. Yet, it remained. Like His his little tale of the wheat and the tares, the two contrasting realms would co-exist until the End, that final crowning of Divine Love.

The response of the old scapegoating order, in dealing with the in-breaking Queendom, proved to be as devious as one would expect from such an entrenched, dogged foe. It's warped, primal genius decided to absorb Yeshua and His radical message. "No sense in fighting it openly, it concluded. "Instead, I'll embrace it by bringing the Nazarene's followers onboard, prior to their deprogramming and domestication." This insidious master stroke both adopted and adapted the emerging *Christian* faith, reinventing it as a sacred tool for the continuance of ritualistic scapegoating and violence, the very essence of *righteous* culture.

The old, sacrificial religion, with its emphasis on blood

offerings and expiation, rushed in to claim the newly sponsored faith's theological high ground. The *Abba* Transcendence of Yeshua was reinvented, under watchful, Roman supervision, as one of the gods of old; those placated through the violent loss of life. The Nazarene's message of an unconditional love that flows freely from Divine Source, was deftly airbrushed into a dualistic decision of *accepting* or *rejecting* His redeeming payment for sin. It proved to be an astute, religious move for culture's ego-based, desire matrix. Skewed desire and its scapegoating mechanism could once again hold sway within the competing worlds of *believer* and *nonbeliever.* The regularly required victim could easily be found outside the Christian tribe, or indeed, from within, in the form of *heretics* and *dissenters*. The most devious tactic devised by this revitalised, mimetic system, was the believer's potential rivalry with Yeshua Himself. By attempting to outdo the Model Saviour in his boundless, *sacrificial love,* the zealous adherent only set in motion a frustrating, religious power play; one in which self-hatred craftily disguised itself as holiness and sainthood.

Yes, Constantine, the Roman emperor who befriended Christianity, was no political or religious fool. By welcoming the irksome Yeshua movement into the affairs of State, he redirected their desire focus away from Spirit Source and back into the cultural mimetic mix of men. Empire birthed empire, a human institution that we still mistakenly perceive as the people of God.

Realising that we move in and out of these two opposing worlds on a daily basis, we now begin to feel a genuine compassion for our fellow-man. Yet all too easily, we can insidiously use our new awareness of the *Queendom* to *scapegoat* those who still don't comprehend it. In doing so, we inadvertently step back into the proud world of culture, with its knowledge-based sense of overarching superiority. The temptation remains for all *enlightened* Yeshua followers to scapegoat the religious or political *other;* a hypocritical act of the highest order, that only Spirit Breath can save us from. Freedom from such a judgemental tendency is, in itself, a definitive sign that we're living in, if only momentarily, the experiential Queendom that Yeshua came to inaugurate.

So what of this alternative Queendom? Where is it to be found within the world of form? Well, the answer, while simple, requires a level of Divine revelation to fully pin it down. For shockingly, the genesis of this brave new world, that culmination of the Ages, lies within. Spirit Breath, our space-time interface with Divine Love, carries deep within it, the fulfilment of Yeshua's Messianic vision. A seed that doesn't desire the Being of another; one containing no metaphysical rivalry nor contagious violence; one that grows into the very image of the Nazarene, the Cosmic Parent's Son, the Man outside Desire.

14

Red Or Blue Pill?

Once we've been drawn into the subliminal desire flow of Divine Love, we have the potential to live as originally planned. This restored way of life is variously referred to as *the Kingdom/Queendom of God, walking in the Spirit, being in Christ, born from above* etc, using the religious vocabulary of the early Christian writings. Yet, is this alternative mode of being just an ethereal dream of no earthly use, or a practical detachment from the tentacles of skewed desire, and its ever present side-kick, the scapegoat mechanism?

Well, in everyday living we tend to move in and out of both possibilities, viz. Culture and Spirit. As we learn to ride the wave of Spirit, we'll begin to spend more time on the board of realigned desire than off it. If and when we do fall off, Divine Love is always on hand to lift us back up from ego's dark depths. Back in the 1980s, Roel Kaptein, a

Dutch pastor and psychologist, providentially gave me his intriguing perspective on our realms of choice. Influenced by the radical, mimetic theory of French thinker and confidante, Rene Girard, Roel proved to be a heaven-sent messenger, one whose brief input kick-started my own psycho-spiritual recovery. I've taken the liberty of adding my own particular twist to some of his shared thoughts on life's two opposing domains, as detailed below.

Culture

The home of humanity's skewed desire system, with its traditional, *scapegoating* safety valves.

Spirit

The sphere where networks of human relationships can exist without *rivalry* and *violence.*

Culture

I don't listen to the *other*, only using conversation to *win* my point. I rival the other with my words.

Spirit

I listen deeply to the other even when their words hurt. There are elements of *truth* in what they say.

Matrix Messiah

Culture

I hunt out *guilty* parties.

Spirit

I focus on my own *responsibilities*.

Culture

I split society into two: the *goodies* and the *baddies*.

Spirit

I take *responsibility* for my own actions.

Culture

I ask pointed questions to *unsettle* the other, in the hope of defeating them.

Spirit

I ask sincere questions, explaining *why* I've asked them, in a state of vulnerability.

Culture

I *assume* that I know the motivations of the other.

Spirit

I *ask* when I'm unsure of another's real meaning, without

any prior assumptions.

Culture

When the other is embarrassed or weakened I *take advantage* and strike.

Spirit

I *respect* another's weakness and vulnerability, as I do my own.

Culture

I *evade* the other's eyes or use mine to put pressure on them.

Spirit

I look into another's eyes, thus revealing my own *vulnerability,* the eyes being the window of my psyche-soul.

Culture

I have *no time* for the other; there are Don Quixote-like battles to be won elsewhere.

Spirit

I am *open* to the *other,* since most of my business is relatively unimportant.

Culture

I *gossip* about the other not present, using their story as a weapon in a power game.

Spirit

I don't do this.

Culture

I *deny* the feelings and impressions of others. My truth is absolute and the judge of all men.

Spirit

I genuinely *hear* others' feelings and impressions. They are real for them and a sincere expression of their psyche-soul.

Culture

I use *divisive, sectarian* language making the other feel insecure.

Spirit

I use *simple* language, words that unite and embrace all humanity.

Culture

I scapegoat others by *moralising*, bringing Divine Love onto my side for greater effect.

Spirit

In moralising, I am *judging* a part of *my own* shadow Self. Therefore, I forgive all aspects of my psyche-soul, just as Divine Love has done.

Culture

I use the Bible and other holy writings to *judge* others. Textual hand grenades are regularly lobbed in the frantic battle for the religious high ground of *rightness*.

Spirit

Scriptural narratives are used as paths into *freedom*, ones that leads away from desire rivalry and into the magnetic flux of Divine alignment.

Culture

My favourite word is *but*. It negates all that I have previously conceded to the *other* in the tit-for-tat power game.

Spirit

I attempt to use the word *and* to link my statements of

personal perception.

Culture
I *don't like* someone, thereby scapegoating them.

Spirit
I can see fragments of my own *wounded psyche* in the other. By forgiving and extending love to my fractured *Self*, I will consequently do the same for the *other*.

Culture
I use *why* questions to imprison myself and others in the regretful dungeons of the past.

Spirit
I ask *where* Spirit is leading me now in the ever present, Divine flow.

Culture
I get really *excited* about things and attempt to convert others to my laser-like enthusiasm regarding the spiritual path.

Spirit
I focus on the *still, small Voice* within, attempting to remain

free in its paradoxical silence.

Culture

I *blame* the other for our relational breakdown.

Spirit

I ask Divine Love for its *perspective* on my relational problems.

Culture

I *thwart* the creativity of others in my power game with them.

Spirit

I *speak well* of the other and their creative gifts, asking what I can *learn* from them.

Culture

I use *strong language* in my forceful attempt to convince the other of the correctness of my position, often calling on the ultimate authority of God to back me up. All swearing is a form of scapegoating.

Spirit

I use *simple words* and as few as possible to express how I feel, even in the most distressing of situations.

Culture
I manipulate the other, albeit sometimes unknowingly. When my *skewed desire goa*l is blocked I become angry, blaming and scapegoating the other.

Spirit
I speak *openly* and *honestly* with the other, happy with their choices when made in freedom, even if I disagree.

Culture
I *worry* about the other, thereby putting myself in a superior, one-up position above them.

Spirit
I have *compassion* for the other, carrying some of their psycho-spiritual pain. It reflects my own level of brokenness. Together, we journey on into the healing experience of Divine Love.

Culture
Others are my *flock,* I am somehow superior to them in the hierarchy of life.

Spirit

I am a part of others. All of us are awakening to the Ultimate Reality of our *union* with Divine Love.

To summarise, Yeshua bar Yosef, has introduced a new possibility into our lives by the release of Sacred Breath; an authentic, counter-cultural Way of Being in the somewhat heady, desire affairs of man. We are now able to move in and out of a new-found freedom, by an act of will. The Nazarene requested, "Your *will* be done on Earth as it is in the heavens". In coming into a wilful realignment with the energy of Divine desire, this prayer is no longer a religious pipe-dream, but a much welcomed and liberating possibility for all of us exhausted by rivalry games.

15

Contrasting Queendom

Once we realise that Yeshua came to expose, and release us from, the hidden dynamic of skewed desire and all its cultural manifestations, we're still not out of the shadowy woods of our fragmented psyche. For the reflex temptation to resist the *old order* and its human agencies, is itself a skewed desire, one that only returns us to the downward spiral of its deadly pull.

Contrary to much religious thought, the *Queendom* of God isn't a counter or contra-cultural reality. Why not? Well, as soon as we set ourselves against the scapegoating system, we inadvertently become its mirror image, thereby remaining a player in its incestuous game. Rather, the in-breaking Queendom that we've glimpsed and been reconnected to, is a contrast culture, one without the foundation stone of rivalling violence.

Unfortunately, religion and politics don't help us with

our new predicament, for they are the very playing fields on which the desire matrix loves to do its thing. Opposing the other, *even* in the name of *equity* and *justice*, is to still partake in the scapegoating game. And let's face it, is there any evidence to date, that a reformist political or religious movement has successfully played its trump card by establishing the utopian Queendom on Earth? Surely, historical events would tragically suggest otherwise. Such is the insidious nature of our adversarial relationships, that the enthusiastic heralds of Yeshua's New World quickly morph into Warring Doubles, those Rivalling Twins who fight for the right to be right. So where does all this leave us? Is our attempt to live in the Queendom of God an ultimately futile exercise? Paradoxically, I believe the answer to be both yes and no. I'd better explain.

The realm of desire freedom, that associated with Divine Love, lies outside our conceptualised, space-time world. Like its Source, we eventually realise that *it just is*. The world to which we awaken each morning, is just another dream, albeit one without a timeless essence; a linear virtual reality of sorts, in which we live and move and appear to have our being. Journeying through this fantastical road trip called life, something of *Other* unexpectedly breaks in from time to time. The psycho-spiritual frequency on which we usually operate, is hijacked by the Divine broadcaster. Spirit Breath, the playful essence of Divine Love, takes pleasure in interrupting our dream-like state, by transmitting timely droplets of Reality into the sleepy airwaves of our conscious mind.

In other words, the Queendom of God is a gifted Reality, one that allows us to live within the space-time Matrix, without having to abide by its scapegoating rules. Tuning into the Divine programme, we are freed from the control of acquisitive desire. Yet, the settings on our internal desire dial are not fixed, remaining open to interference from the multifarious desire fields that we encounter in everyday living. So how can we consistently enjoy the radical freedom that Yeshua came to deliver? Well, here are a few simple tips for our consideration:

Find time for Regular Prayer or Meditation
Consciously being in the Silent Presence, the mimetic desire field of Divine Love, develops an experiential communion that surpasses words and concepts.

Follow the Way

Responding to the gentle, imitative magnetism of Spirit Breath's energy and advances.

Allow Healing to come

Healing, the ditching of psychological desire attachments and their accompanying addictions, in order to enjoy the freedom of living outside the pressure cooker of skewed desire, is the very freedom of Yeshua himself. Divine Love will organise a personal consultation, giving us the choice of proceeding or running back into our psycho-spiritual shell.

Expose oneself to the weak and broken

In these dear souls, the scapegoats of our go-getting society, we will encounter the Presence of Divine Love. The Queendom of God lies close to the broken and rejected within our lemming-like communities.

Worship as much as possible

Reaching out, in awe and wonder, to the Source from which we've emerged, initiates a Divine flow, one that empowers and reassures. Best outside the sphere of cultural religion, in the midst of Nature and the solitude of the soul.

Experience Community

Our contact with others on the Way; those open to the regular approaches of Divine Love is a great psycho-spiritual resource. The two or three of Yeshua's community model is all that's needed to draw down the Divine Presence. Honesty and vulnerability is all that is required.

Finally, a little explanation those of you for whom the word, *"Kingdom,"* denotes the realm of Divine Love. For the sake of simplicity, I've decided to use the alternative term, *"Queendom,"* throughout this work, since the ancient Hebrew, and Aramaic nouns for this Reality are feminine in gender. No goddess worship is inferred by my thoughts, but rather a focus on accurate semantics and an emphasis on the often neglected, nurturing nature of Divine Love.

16

"Earth Calling Heaven!"

In the previous chapter, we explored the contrasting nature of the Queendom of God and its psycho-spiritual *otherness*. I now wish to examine in detail one of the practices that can help us maintain our experience of this transcendent, liberating realm, viz. prayer or meditation. Let me start though, by making a subtle, but vitally important distinction between these two aspects of our internal communication with Reality.

Meditation is a much practised, historical technique, one that helps us to bypass the conflicting voices of our fragmented psyche-soul's sub-personalities. The human spirit, our divine spark, has the innate ability to filter out our raging ego discussions and listen to itself in the stillness of silence. Those who regularly meditate experience a profound, albeit temporary, sense of Oneness with the created order. In an Eastern Monist view of Ultimate

Reality, this Oneness is interpreted as the Divine, with each of us a particular facet of the "All is God". May I respectfully, but perhaps controversially, suggest that this much sought after connection with *Cosmic Consciousness,* is none other than the individual's discovery of their own spirit-Self, their *I am,* their *me* birthed outside space-time.

I believe meditation to be a much valued gateway, one through which many pass on their Way to the Divine City. Yet, some practitioners of its stillness techniques, tend to set up camp just through the gate, claiming that the ultimate secret of the Cosmos has been discovered. A mysterious new world has most certainly been revealed to the ardent meditator, yet one whose Ultimate Source still remains somewhat hidden and silent.

Prayer, on the other hand, although sharing many characteristics with meditation, has one clear distinction. In prayer, the *I am* spark doesn't sit alone, but in the Presence of an Other. During meditation, the human spirit alone communicates with the stilled psyche-soul. During prayer, intimate communication is established between the Divine Voice and the psyche-soul via *the channel* of our *I am,* spirit-Self. The difference is extremely subtle but in Reality, worlds apart.

The meditator sees themself as an intricate part of the Cosmic Consciousness, whilst the prayer practitioner sees their communication as a conversational *union* with original Source. In other words, prayer is a *relationship* based communication whereas meditation is a solitary Self Awareness exercise, albeit an extremely valuable one. Unfortunately, these differing psycho-spiritual exercises tend to fall into two distinct metaphysical camps.

Prayer is generally the preferred practice for those of a monotheistic bent, e.g. Christians, Jews, Muslims etc whilst meditation is the favoured technique for those of a Monist bent viz. Buddhists, some Hindu schools of thought and many Mind, Body, Spirit philosophies. Yet, as a follower of Yeshua bar Yosef, I reckon that both practices are essential for a truly integrated spiritual life. Many of us raised in traditional religious circles, no matter what the particular brand, were taught, at an early age, to *rattle off* set prayers, usually before going to sleep. A rote learnt, religious duty; one to ensure that our Divine Protector didn't grow a little forgetful by leaving us exposed to the night-time powers of darkness!

Much adult prayer remains motivated by these childish fears, our programmed forebodings that distort our perception of Divine Love and its desire for relational intimacy. Induced guilt and shame often play a major role in our infantile approach to the One to whom we regularly dispatch our fear-driven request lists. Doubting that we're accepted, let alone loved, we tend to avoid snuggling up to our Divine Source, just in case we receive a sacred *clip on the ear*. In contrast, true prayer or conversational communion with our Cosmic Parent, is one of the most precious side effects of a Spirit Breath encounter.

Meditation, on the other hand, is an effective technique for stilling the psychological storms that often rage within our somewhat frantic soul space. The key benefit of this psycho-spiritual exercise is the revelation that we're more than our ego, our wounded, deeply fragmented psyche-soul which stubbornly hogs the steering wheel of our space-time existence. Our divine spark, the human spirit, always dwells in a place of peace and equilibrium. The discovery that such a quiet *presence* exists within the noisy community of our inner world, can greatly diminish the pressures on our troubled psyche-souls; an authentic *me* that appears to connect with Divine Source itself.

In times of great stress, when we're often unable to pray due to the confusion of our inner chatter, detachment, followed by a meditative focus on the *I am* within, can surprisingly bring fast results, viz. a restored calm and quiet sanity. From there, we can once more tune into the Voice beyond, the Voice of the Beloved, the One calling us into the Garden of Divine Presence.

In the next chapter we'll explore the Nazarene's model prayer, commonly known as "The Lord's Prayer", from a radical, new perspective, viz. that of Girardian desire theory.

17

The Yeshua Prayer

Previously, I suggested that prayer is one of the four main practices by which we can retain something of the in breaking *Queendom of God,* in our day-to-day lives. Unfortunately prayer has been interpreted by our religious traditions as a somewhat spiritless duty, something we *should do* in order to keep the Divine happy. Strangely though, it's actually the other way around. Prayer is one way to keep *ourselves* happy, by experiencing the gift of desire detachment as granted by Divine Source.

As a young lad, raised in the religious heartland of Northern Ireland, I was regularly drilled in *The Lord's Prayer*, the recorded prayer of Yeshua bar Yosef. This demo-model of man-God chat was, more than likely, a one time, off the cuff example for his disciples benefit. Anyway, along with thousands of other rote-taught, Irish youngsters, I could rattle off this wee prayer at the drop of a big black

Bible. Years later, as a high school teacher, I'd regularly cringe as the *Our Father* was chanted aloud by hundreds of pupils during our morning religious assemblies, in the same dreary manner that generations of pupils had done before them. The black humour of this pseudo-sacred, daily ritual was aptly illustrated by the highly predictable, yet ultra-thespian delivery of the prayer's opening line, by my duty-bound, unbelieving headmaster. In light of such repetitive, religious roundabouts, perhaps the ban on prayer in American schools isn't such a bad thing after all!

Let's consider Yeshua's familiar prayer from the relatively unknown perspective of mimetic desire theory. Hopefully, such an approach will reveal previously hidden truths and the practical benefits that flow from them. But first, please allow me the metaphysical liberty of renaming the *Lord's Prayer* as *Yeshua's Realignment Prayer*. I think you'll understand why as we go along.

Our Father in the heavens

The *Abba* god of the Nazarene dwells in the transcendent realms of Ultimate Reality. As a result, this Cosmic Parent-Source lies totally outside the manipulative power plays of our desire-skewed ego. We can't rival such a

One because He is altogether *Other*. He simply acts as an external mediator of its own nature, viz. Unconditional Love. This Divinity always authenticates us from a *safe distance*, one lying infinitely beyond the reach of our vampire-like lust for another's being.

May your name be held holy

The little word, *holy,* tends to freak many of us out, due to its all too common association with the carrot and stick approach of much religious thought. Yet, its root meaning simply suggests *"a setting apart for a special purpose"*. The name of *God*, no matter how we attempt to phrase it, is essentially, a reflection of the Divine essence. Thankfully, this *Otherness* can't be contaminated by our efforts to fashion it in our own image, to transform it into a *scapegoater* like us. Rather, Yeshua's Cosmic Parent is the God of the *scapegoats,* a vital lesson that our cultural, religious mindset quickly chooses to forget.

Your Queendom come

This God realm, one free of skewed desire, is made available to us all as a gift. It can't be earned, not even by our zealously pious efforts to manifest it here on Earth. It flows from Divine Love and to Divine Love it shall return.

Your will be done

Surrendering our dysfunctional desire centre to Divine Love, we automatically come into a mimetic flow with its *all-consuming desire* or *will*. We now act as a spiritual router of sorts for the Divine nature, a transmitter of Spirit desire into this space-time matrix. Divine words and acts of Source compassion will pour through us, thereby revealing the Queendom, that realm without rivalling desire and contagious violence.

On earth, as it is in the heavens

Within the transcendent sphere of Source, no rivalry exists. The *"Satan"* or *"Adversary"*, that personification of desire conflict and its accompanying scapegoat mechanism, only operates in the space-time illusion of ego consciousness. Outside the shadowlands of human existence, all created beings are in total mimesis with Ultimate Reality. As we allow Divine Love to manifest itself through our reintegrated, realigned psyche-souls, a little colony of the Queendom is firmly established in our little piece of virtual earth.

Give us today tomorrow's bread

Once we have tasted Divine Love, via an experience of Spirit-Breath, our desire needs change into those that can be supplied by Source. We no longer need to fight for our necessities, for all that we require is freely given. Our *ego hunter gatherer* can be given its dismissal notice in the workplace of Being. The bread of tomorrow's Queendom, that Divine Presence which will ultimately consume space-time, is available for us today, in the *eternal now*.

And forgive us our transgressions

To *transgress* is to live outside the flow and influence of Divine Love, to return to the mimetic jungle of desire rivalry. Forgiveness is the relational default setting of the Divine nature. Our *asking* for forgiveness isn't a desperate plea for mercy to an unconvinced deity. Rather, it's an honest acknowledgement that, for whatever reason, we've temporarily stepped out of our Queendom home. In other words, we're informing our Cosmic Parent that our prodigal psyche-soul is once more leaving the dualistic world of rivalry and returning to the unified cradle of its Being.

As we've forgiven those who have transgressed against us

Once we realise how the scapegoat mechanism operates, we can no longer make anyone the guilty party by clamouring for their psycho-spiritual death. As rampant scapegoaters, our motto of choice was always, "It's either them or us." Now however, we see things more clearly, wishing that everyone will awaken to the experience of Divine realignment. Still, only Divine Love can change the desire settings of our fellow travellers. Our role is no longer to condemn others from a position of ego superiority, but to draw alongside them as recovering desire junkies.

And do not put us to the test

Keep us close to the magnetic, mimetic field of Spirit-Breath. May we not wander aimlessly into the gravitational pull of a potential *model obstacle* or *monstrous double*. May we not have to trip over a human *scandalon* or *stumbling block* in order to realise that we've moved away from the desire centre of your Love.

But deliver us from the evil one

Keep us from participating in the scapegoating mob of human culture, the *Adversary* who attempts to draw us into the battle for metaphysical Being. Such a system of inter-personal relationships is indeed *evil,* or to be more accurate, *broken and unfit for purpose*. We can stand firm in our freedom from acquisitive desire as we meet its personification in the approaching rivalry of another.

For yours is the Queendom, the power and the glory

The Queendom of desire freedom has its source in the Divine Nature. It isn't something that we conjure up through religious or spiritual self-effort. Rather, it's a one-way infusion of Spirit that draws us back into the liberty of God Himself. This transcendent realm bursts with a dynamic ability to achieve its goals, based on the creative rights of its, *I Am That I Am,* Source. Birthed in the Light of pure Being, our contact with this invading Queendom inspires awe and worship, a resonance with the *One* lying beyond the ego-based limitations of human experience.

For ever and ever

The Reality of Divine Love and its Being is something that the illusions of space-time cannot determine nor control. Our Source Parent just is, both inside and outside the reach of our human perception. It's a living, pulsating Presence that has no beginning and no end, the timeless womb to which we shall all return.

In praying, we're tuning into a mimetic desire field, both for ourselves and others. We're standing down our psycho-spiritual flood defences to allow Divine Love to have its *Way*, its *desire;* the communion of man and God. Our *invocation* is responding to a pre-ordained, magnetic attraction, one that draws us into the Mystery of the Ages, our place of Divine Rest. As we pray, much is going on behind the screen of our rational consciousness, stirrings of Spirit of which we aren't fully aware. Yet some day, I reckon, all will become *very, very* clear!

18

The Spirit-Soul Reunion Waltz

Learning to live outside the skewed, mimetic desire field, is a process; one that takes place under the gracious, but determined tutelage of *Other*. Gently nudging us towards the fullness of our new-found freedom, Spirit Breath is quite content to work within the boundaries and restrictions of our space-time world. Even the early followers of Yeshua, folk as *screwed-up* as ourselves, took a while to finally get the message, it being all to easy for them to relapse into the old sacrificial paradigms of their religious upbringing. At times, just following Yeshua into Divine mimesis proved too simple an ask for their still recovering egos. I guess we are no different. Perhaps an answer to these unsettling inconsistencies in our new life lies in the process of *psyche reintegration* or *inner healing*. So, let's explore the nature of this restorative therapy, one regularly prescribed and performed by Divine Love during our journey into experiential wholeness.

Our skewed desire centre is the cause of much inner and outer pain. Absorbing the hypnotic power of another's desire, with all its consequential rivalry and violence, psycho-spiritual wounding is almost certain to occur. The *survival mode* psyche-soul that ensues, with its defensive mission of warding off future rivals, is paradoxically the source of our future pain; *fight, flight* or *freeze* being its tripartite, fear-fuelled action plan. We wander through this threatening veil of tears, anxiously expecting a personal attack at any second. Yes, it's hard to be at peace in the matrix trenches of *inter-personal rivalry.*

Yet, onto our tortuous, inner path steps *One* who calls us into the imitative freedom of *desire realignment;* the *Source* of all desire energy, the *Other* whose transmission frequency finally rings true. Such a dramatic *encounter* is our first experience of *Inner* Healing with a capital H. The psycho-spiritual effects of our contact with the Divine Model, One who simply asks us to follow, are often quite dramatic. An authentic, born from above connection can be established, one that reignites the Divine spark of spirit as our guide back into wholeness and psychological freedom.

Following such a *conversion* or *awakening experience,*

we tend to float on a euphoric psycho-spiritual cloud for a while, before returning to earth with a bump. Once landed, we begin to realise that the old mimetic desire matrix hasn't gone away, for it still exerts a measure of gravitational pull on our recovering psyche. It's at this point that some of us *give up the Ghost,* returning as disillusioned pilgrims to our old mimetic paths, convinced that our transcendent encounter was merely an *emotional* experience, one that ultimately proved fruitless. Others, those who simply choose to observe the paradoxes of their inner world, eventually hear a *still, small Voice,* one that whispers *healing* to the family of their wounded selves.

Healing is the gradual reintegration of our psyche's fragmented sub-personalities via the experiential embraces of Divine Love. The decommissioning and reunification of these little psyche-based attack dogs, is the liberating outcome of our continuing union with Source. Usually, such a therapeutic process begins with a dramatic, Spirit Breath intervention, one that tends to follow a debilitating, transpersonal crisis. Thankfully though, it continues on in a somewhat less dramatic fashion as, one by one, each of our little wounded *Selves* is tenderly targeted by the Divine therapist.

The ups and downs of our new life, like the rhythmic waves on some restorative Ocean, carry us ever closer to the psycho-spiritual wholeness that we internally crave, that *Divine Bosom* as experienced by mystics throughout the ages. Slowly but surely, we begin to see our life experiences from the Divine perspective; a step by step journey of healing and reintegration, rather than the frantic survival battle as scripted by our ego pain.

All psycho-spiritual healing is a form of realignment; the reunification of our psyche-soul with Divine Love and its infectious Desire, known in religious circles as *the* Will of God. Now, for many of us, the latter stirs up terrifying images of a Divine Controller, one who dictates what we can and cannot do. Yet, such a legalistic caricature is false, for *Divine Desire* is the ultimate, liberating energy surge, a river of contentment that carries us along on its orgasmic flow of joyful *Being*. Living in mimesis with Divine Love isn't the proverbial, religious endurance test that many believe it to be. Instead, it's a welcome and much needed release from the ever present rivalry of the human desire matrix.

Our defensive sub-personalities, the little soldier boys and girls who man our ego fortress, are drawn, one-by-one, out of their pain-fuelled isolation, and into the community of the Beloved, that cherished Divine Union planted within the garden of Self. Wisdom carefully selects Her prodigal target of choice. The tell-tale sign of selection is the immediate kickback of the sub-personality in question. Like some tantrum-charged infant, it goes off on one, unwittingly manifesting its controlling emotion, instinctively fearing that its time may have come come.

So what is the key to this therapeutic reintegration of our inner self? Well, our sub-personalities prefer to operate from the dark depths of the lower unconscious, that psychic cellar where our past traumas and associated wounds are stored. Spirit's healing aim is to release each sub-personality into the Light of consciousness, where it can be embraced by Unconditional Love. Here its valuable defensive role in our psychic survival is affirmed, but no longer allowed to dominate. Following such a Divine encounter, the sources of our inner angst are miraculously transformed, like the Gadarene demoniac who was found sitting and in his right mind, after his brush with Yeshua's laser like Love. Once we come to know our sub-personality, its origin, character and modus operandi, its destructive power quickly dissipates as it willingly lays itself at the feet of Divine Love

Amazingly, the dominant characteristics of each of our delinquent sub-personalities can be realigned and recruited into the service of Divine Love. In doing so another nail can be well and truly hammered into the coffin of our psychic fragmentation. Such a process, one that continues through our length of days, lies at the very heart of our *inner healing*, the very *essence* of our salvation.

19

Helper Or Healer?

We've just looked at the vital role *healing* plays in rooting us within the psycho-spiritual realm known as the Queendom of God. However, maintaining our freedom from the effects of skewed desire and its subliminal matrix is a life time's task. For even such a vital and wonderful gift as healing, can be commandeered by our remaining sub-personalities as weapons in their competitive power games. A vital lesson perhaps, for all us zealous helper healers.

The new world of Divine Love is a world of liberty and wholeness, one where the inner contradictions of our fragmented ego are a thing of the past. Psychic reintegration, under the therapeutic oversight of Holy Breath, is the fruit of our new awareness, an awareness of how things really are. Disengaged from the swirling desire field that surrounds us, we discover our new desires to be those of Divine Love itself, viz. the desire to be and *to* reignite *being* in all who cross our path.

Yet, following our born from above enlightenment experience, we soon discover our fragmented ego to be a much more cunning opponent than we first imagined. How come? Well, it immediately strikes back by fashioning us into one of God's little helpers. Shocking as it may seem, *helping* is *not* the same as *healing*; a painful, yet vital truth for all us moral zealots to discover. Helping always lies within the arena of culture, an ever present aspect of our space-time power-games. Deeply embedded within our dysfunctional psyche, helping is generally accepted as a good thing and yet, it's an insidiously clever way of maintaining power over others, those who unknowingly become our scapegoat victims.

Our manipulation of the needs of others is an intense rivalry game, one poorly disguised as caring *concern*. Yet, concern itself is always the clear give-away, revealing as it does our superior attitude towards the one in need. The more *professional* our help becomes, the more dishonest our supposed mission of mercy turns out to be; a manipulation of the *patient* in order to make ourselves a living. Like some giant whirlpool, the professional care industry destroys the face of the Nazarene in the needy one, by sucking it down into the depths of our institutionalised compassion.

Of course, many of us have already entered the caring professions. On my more thoughtful days I often wonder why, but the answer to that one must wait for another time. Clearly, as professionals we *can* still operate out of freedom, the freedom of the Queendom, but it's always an uphill struggle; one against the top-down victimisation that views the other as a patient, client or, even worse, a statistic. In the eyes of the Nazarene they are no less than our brother or sister.

Healing, on the other hand, seems to be somewhat spontaneous. Unexpectedly meeting another, one who walks in desire freedom, can instantaneously jump start our own psycho-spiritual battery. We just know that this healer is free, acting as channel for the dynamic power of Other. I suspect that many of Yeshua's healing encounters with those sick in body and mind, followed such a therapeutic path. For once Divine Love hits us, a heavenly rewiring occurs, one that returns both body and psyche-soul to the default settings of Spirit, viz. order and wholeness. So how can we tell if we're a helper or a healer? Well, here a few healing characteristics that may help us self-diagnose:

A healer is never busy, occupying an almost timeless space with the other. Such a therapeutic space is filled with mutual respect, for the healer sees themself in the face of the other.

A healer doesn't invade the other's psychic space in a violently superior, "I know better" manner.

A healer draws the other out of their condition rather than forcing them to leave it.

A healer ignores cultural differences by creating a safe space, where the two, in some mysterious psychic way, become one, if only for an instant.

So how does healing take place? Well, it's the welcome result of blocked desire channels being reopened within our psyche Many who require healing, are in the paralysing grip of rivalrous Model Obstacle or Monstrous Double relationships, ones that quickly take their destructive toll on both psyche and body. The healer, in drawing the wounded one into their own relational freedom, unblocks the log jams of frustrated desire, resulting in a healthy spatial mimesis in the life of the other. When *non acquisitive* desire flows freely between both parties, a channel of Divine Love is established, whereby both are saved from the debilitating effects of any previous or potential rivalries.

As we've already seen, spontaneous healing can occur when any two people meet. Indeed, all personal encounters comprise a level of desire exchange, either one that heals or one that enslaves. When meeting in freedom, amazing things can transpire between two psyche-souls. The miracle of mutual healing can regularly manifest itself, once we've given up our old scapegoating ways, the sacrificial blame game that previously kept us at each other's throats.

Healing also occurs within a *group* context when we encounter folk who collectively live and move in mimetic freedom. We're drawn into their communal core, viz. desire detachment and lack of cultural power games, thereby experiencing a little colony of the Queendom on Earth. Of course, such healing groups are rare, and once found, treasures to embrace. Often lying outside the strong, cultural desire field of organised religion, they tend to comprise *the walking wounded*, those dear souls damaged by a prior zealous involvement in the flawed metaphysical endeavours of their youth. Wounded healers indeed.

20

Divine Resonance

An inner sense of having *been* healed, at least partially, is one of the tell-tale signs that we're living in the freedom realm, known as the Queendom of God. Another is the desire to worship, an English term, one that immediately invokes joy or dread, depending on our religious background. In the Western religious tradition of the past two millennia, worship is almost entirely synonymous with community singing aimed at the Divine. Theologically laden, 18th century revivalist hymns, haunting Gregorian chants or trendy new rock and roll worship songs, those ascribed to Spirit, but usually copyrighted to an ever-prospering singer songwriter, are globally offered up to Source, each and every, Sunday morning. Worship music is now big business with hordes of spiritually frustrated folk frantically searching for an authentic *Divine touch* via their ipods. Here though, I'm going to step back from our institutionalized model of community ritual, and examine worship from a *desire based* perspective. By focusing on Divine-Resonance, I'll hopefully shed some new light on Yeshua's radical words to the man-hungry, yet paradoxically religious, Samaritan woman at the well.

"The Father is seeking those to worship Him in spirit and in truth."

Firstly, let me reassure you that the *Father* or *Cosmic Parent* isn't some great, big, Heavenly Narcissist, one who continually scours the world of men for besotted admirers. *"Worship me, my lucky creatures, for I have ego needs of Divine proportions!"* No, Divine Love is intrinsically at peace with its own boundless sense of Being. Its spilling over into creative mode isn't the desperate action of a self-doubting, Greek god, one in need of our constant reassurance, but rather, a manifestation of its infinite joy, a sharing of its essential essence. The direction of Divine desire flow is ever only one way, viz. towards the *other;* a disarming invitation into the peace-filled Union of God and man. Thus all requests for worship, as recorded in both Jewish and Christian scriptures, are based on this totally *unselfish* premise, contrary to the misinterpretations of much religious thought. No, Divine Love draws us *into* worship as a means of healing and realignment, not as the desired end of some eternally manipulative power trip.

Yeshua conversed with His new, Samaritan friend in Aramaic, the language of the common people in first century Palestine. Surprisingly, the Aramaic word translated into English as worship, is the term seged, a verb meaning *to* bow, surrender or adore. Not much hearty hymn singing or happy clappy-fuelled dancing there then! Of course, within Hebrew culture there *were* designated occasions for such boisterous expressions, albeit as reflex acts of letting off steam following military victories, those supposedly engineered by their tribal God, Yahweh. OK then, so how does seged relate to mimetic desire and the maintenance of our Divinely gifted freedom? Well, let's take a closer look at each of its root meanings in turn.

To Bow

In Middle Eastern culture, bowing down was a physical acknowledgement that one was in the presence of a greater being, such as a ruler, or more importantly, a god. In Jewish folk tales of angelic appearances, the poor old angel's first task was always to get their traumatised human subject back on their feet; in other words, to stop them participating in the act of seged. Now, many of us have rediscovered a new spirituality of Oneness, as promoted by certain Eastern philosophies, and yet, this valuable, Monist revelation can birth a refusal to bow down to anyone or anything. The persuasive argument goes something like this: *"If we're all manifestations of the Divine, then clearly there is no-one greater to bow down to."* Such is the subtle, but important difference between pantheist (All are God) and panentheistic (All are in God) world views, my own take on the underlying mystery of things being the latter.

Mimetic desire appears to have been pre-wired into the human psyche by Divine Source. In its dysfunctional form, viz. *skewed desire,* we absorb and unconsciously imitate the desires of our fellow man. This infectious process, while initially delivering the drug-like *buzz* of desire infatuation, usually ends in tears, disillusionment and relational breakdown. In contrast, the Queendom realm, as ably demonstrated by the Nazarene, focuses our psychic desire centre solely on Source, the One who birthed us in the great Cosmic Dance of Creation. The realignment and reintegration of our psyche-soul's desire receptors, follow an encounter with Transcendent *Other*, via the Presence of

Spirit Breath. To experience Other is to automatically bow down; for we just can't stop ourselves after such a primal reintroduction.

To Surrender

An act of surrender implies that a prior struggle has taken place in the sensory soul realm. Ego, comprising our vigilante group of defensive *sub-personalities*, has fought long and hard to protect us from the imaginary threat of annihilation or *non being*. When unconditional love appeared forever out of reach, following the traumatic events of infancy, these fragmented, psycho-spiritual enforcers exploded onto our internal scene, promising, 'Never Again.' Our little army of 'me' now sits on a permanent war footing, ready to protect us from any further psychological pain and victimisation. Operating a first strike policy on those threatening to become our next Model Obstacle or relational stumbling block, our ego task force shows no mercy. Thankfully, into such a fear-fuelled war zone comes Divine Source, a benign Presence that offers us all a way out, viz. its own *Unconditional Love*, as it was originally meant to be. Like the few, hidden, Japanese soldiers who *fought on* for decades after the end of

World War 2, our hyper-diligent sub-personalities are loath to surrender and face up to the truth of Ultimate Reality, viz. that all psycho-spiritual hostilities are well and truly over. Once these subconscious *soldier selves* are lovingly led by Spirit into the Light of Consciousness, surrendering their gift of Will to the now trusted Other, a vital transformation takes place; a psycho-spiritual airlift out of our internalized war zone and into the peace filled realm of Divine acceptance.

To Adore

Let's face it, adoration is a great relief for the wounded psyche. Having spent years hooked on all sorts of desire objects, playing their deadly, gravitational games, it's good to get off the acquisitive treadmill and finally stare at *Reality*. Adoration is simply our conscious co-operation with the desire pull of Divine Love, as it finally reels us in like an exhausted salmon. Thankfully, as the prize catch, we aren't placed in the stagnant pool of dutiful religion, but in the boundless, free-flowing, Waters of Spirit Breath. Yes, adoration is that reflex state of shock that follows our unexpected hijacking by Transcendent Source. Like some rehoused puppy snuggled up beside its new master, we can't take our spiritual eyes off the One who came looking for us, the One who has saved us from our imprisoning, mimetic state.

So, how can we remain authentic in our acts of seged? Well, the thirsty Rabi had a few suggestions for us to ponder. They are as follows:

In Spirit Breath - Ruha

Only Spirit Breath or *Ruha* (Aramaic), can magnetically draw our wandering, fragmented psyche back into the alignment of Divine Resonance. Once there, we're surprised to discover that the desires of Spirit Source itself, surge into our restored, psychic reservoirs via our own spirit spark. Both spirit and psyche-soul now appear to vibrate with the same desire frequency, a resonance birthed in the Divine Will. Previously, we've considered how religion operates in the realm of fragmented self or *ego*, frantically searching for love where it can't be found, viz., in the scapegoating of the other. Spirit Breath, on the other hand, knows nothing of such rivalry and striving, for She is the One who returns us to the *Innocence of the Garden.* Learning to step out of our psychic chatter into a stream of higher consciousness, one where Spirit is only too happy to commune, is the skill of true worship.

In Truth ~Sherara

In Western religious thought, we are obsessed with Truth as a set of right beliefs or, more disturbingly, supposed facts. Thankfully, the Eastern take on Truth or Sherara (Aramaic) is not so restricting. To the Samaritan woman, Yeshua's phrase would have suggested that which liberates and opens up new possibilities, that which vigorously acts in keeping with Universal Harmony. It's simply what leads a person in the right direction at the right time, into an agreeable equilibrium with all. Truth always projects us into our purpose. In other words, it will consistently usher us back into a subliminal imitation of the Divine desire. The evidence of such a life-changing mimetic correction is, of course, unconditional love, that intimate shared expression of the Divine Nature.

Back in 1987, after leaving institutional religion, I'd regularly bump into old Christian associates. *"So where are you worshiping now?"* was often their first enquiry, one smeared with smatterings of a pseudo-brotherly concern. *"Everywhere and nowhere,"* was my reflex response; an answer mischievously tinged with a tiny drop of Irish sarcasm that my zealous religious inquisitor rarely picked up on. Today, if faced with the same loaded question, I'd respectfully reply, *"Simply somewhere where I can bow down, surrender and adore the liberating Breath of Spirit and its whispers of desire Purpose."* For me, that's walking my wee black doggie against the mystical backdrop of Nature. How about you?

21

The Walking Wounded

In this final chapter, I wish to consider the vital role human community plays in keeping us, the *walking wounded*, plugged into the liberation of the Divine Queendom. First, let me start by stating that a faith group is not necessarily a community, nor a community, a faith group. In our 21st century world, we're surrounded by a swirling mass of recruitment groups, all flashing their pseudo-community credentials. Yet, if we join such a pre-packaged, plastic flock. we can still feel lonely and largely unacknowledged in the mind of its frantic, self-defining activities

So then, what *are* the tell-tale signs of genuine *spiritual community*? Well, to answer that let's head back to 1st century Palestine. There, Yeshua bar Yosef, the Nazarene prophet-teacher, followed the Eastern spiritual practice of calling a group of followers or apprentices. Like many before Him, His aim was to draw the selected, motley crew into His own spirituality and experience of Divine Love. In other words, the Galilean was recalibrating their skewed desire settings by simply acting as a Model of both Divinity and aligned Humanity. The overwhelming desire flux that issued from the charismatic prophet drew them into a laser-like focus on Divine Source.

By living with Him 24-7, His followers unwittingly realigned their own metaphysical desire goals, for *mimetic desire* operates in the subliminal realms of the *lower unconscious*. They *caught* their love for God off their Model Master, like some *benign virus* passed on through human contact. The experiment, like all spiritual endeavours, certainly had its low points, as the old imitative rivalries regularly resurfaced. James and John, the aptly named Sons of Thunder jostled for positions of power, while Simon Peter attempted to block his Model Master's Jerusalem destiny. Yet, on the whole, these sincere men and women slowly learned to see human affairs in the context of Yeshua's Cosmic Parent, the all-encompassing Source of Unconditional Love.

Today, as we follow the Nazarene into the magnetic field of Divine Love, we discover, much to our surprise, that we're never really alone; for those who've also survived a transpersonal crisis often travel alongside us on the Way. His challenging, timeless call to dispense with acquisitive desire and return Home, will always be heard by those who've hit rock bottom. The prophet-teacher even promised that where two or three are gathered *into* His *Name*, He'd be somehow present. Certainly a most catchy, psycho-spiritual pledge, but what exactly *does it mean*?

Is the Spirit of the Nazarene necessarily present when a few, or indeed, countless thousands of His followers gather together on a Sunday morning under the Christian banner, in small, wooden preaching stations or ornate, cross laden cathedrals? I believe not. Perhaps I'd better explain.

The most controversial name applied to Yeshua bar Yosef, the *"I am who I will be"*, the somewhat mystical name of the Jewish divinity Yahweh, may hold a hidden clue. This summative expression of Divine Being suggests a total Self-sufficiency, a *fullness* that lacks nothing, viz. a state of absolute detachment from acquisitive desire. So, by inviting us to collectively *come into* His name, the Nazarene is promising us an experience of His own Being.. By absorbing our Model"s desire settings we discover that, in the company of two or three similarly infected souls, we'll experience Oneness, a Oneness that reflects the Divine Union itself? Meeting together, under a religious label of our choice, doesn't guarantee the intimacy of Source Presence, for that is reserved for the community of the *walking wounded*.

It's important to remember that that we can find ourselves involved in one of two forms of community, viz. *quasi* community or *organic* community. Let's have a look at each in turn.

Quasi-Community

This group of individuals appears, to all intents and purposes, to be the *real deal*. A committed group of folk who share a common vision and purpose, often under the guidance of a strong charismatic leader or a centuries old tradition. Both the structure and underlying ethos of such a group permeate its regular get-togethers, providing individual members with a strong sense of security, but at the cost of an imprisoning subliminal conformity. In other words, a quasi-community's identity and function is cultural, resting on the defining foundation stones of myth, ritual, law and structure.

Now, it has to be said that many faith groups fall into

this particular category, functioning as the unconscious counterfeits of Yeshua's *two or three*. For at their heart, quasi-communities are gathering of *scapegoaters*, those who define their identity by *who they aren't*. Behind their public image, the psycho-spiritual settings of such a group are usually calibrated for defence, revealing a level of emotional dishonesty, one built upon a subconscious bedrock of reactionary fear.

Organic Community

Organic community takes root in the soil of human frailty and brokenness. It's a network of flawed, but honest individuals who've had their desire centre shaken to the core by a devastating transpersonal crisis. Suffering from an all too raw psycho-spiritual pain, these battered individuals cry out for being and belonging, ultimately finding it in the scarred faces of their fellow man. Such a vulnerable collective is a gathering of *scapegoats*, those selected for victimhood by an external quasi-community, or alternatively, by a debilitating self-condemnation within. Paradoxically, their social rejection tends to unite them in the shared space of *aloneness* and *relational drought*.

Within organic community, acquisitive desire lies dead

and buried, for the ego games of quasi- community cannot survive in the all pervasive Presence of Divine Love. Thankfully, such a collection of folk isn't an excuse for a whining pity party, or a self-righteous, holy huddle, but rather a *safe space* for psycho-spiritual renewal and ongoing enlightenment. Organic community provides the catalyst for self-forgiveness and the forgiveness of our relational Model Obstacles, those who have caused us to stumble in the rivalry games of our past.

In such an overlooked, yet sublime setting, the healing Presence of Divine Love, as embodied in the Nazarene, is happy to hang out. Honesty, is its only prerequisite for permanent residence within the ragamuffin band of broken humanity, and I suspect that even that is a gift. With egos disengaged, the flow of Spirit Breath can miraculously provide mutual healing, as brokenness touches brokenness. In such a communal context, Yeshua's last meal now makes some kind of sense; a broken body shared with its life blood poured out; the Presence of the *Broken Healer* in the company of His *broken humanity*.

I reckon that Yeshua purposely chooses *"two or three"* as the ideal gathering for the revelation of Divine Presence. The larger a group, the less likely it's going to be a safe space in which to disclose our inner world, especially our unhealed wounds. Let's be frank, more people usually means more masks, more unwanted ego to ego engagements. Like two dogs sniffing each other out, we subliminally examine each others trust credentials before opting for a level of vulnerability, one with the inherent possibility of further psychological pain. When authentic community occurs, a mutual trust will have already evolved, a deep empathic respect for each member's inner wounds. Contrastingly, the danger of pseudo-radical, hierarchical groups, those in which vulnerability and openness to pyramidal leadership is expected without reciprocation, is a recipe for psycho-spiritual disaster; a certain one-way trip to abusive control and eventual disillusionment.

So, how do we go about finding organic community among the hustle and bustle of our daily lives? Well thankfully, I reckon that Divine Love has it all preplanned and under control. Rather than scurrying around, looking for a safe shelter in the religious marketplace of Christendom or any other faith brand, why not relax and give ourselves a break. It's important to remember that the god of Yeshua isn't looking for our commitment to a group.

Instead, Divine Source encourages us to let go of ego control, to surrender to its all-consuming, liberating Love.

As we take such steps of trust, others will unexpectedly join us along the Way, those to heal and be healed by. Some fellow travellers stay with us for years, others for a shorter period of time, but all temporarily. A truly *organic* community, one birthed in the radical discovery of mimetic freedom.

Epilogue

Thank you reader, for accompanying me in my literary exploration of the *desire matrix*, that invisible network of control in which we live and move and search for being. Half way through, we were introduced to the Nazarene, Yeshua bar Yosef, who perhaps more than anyone else in human history, saw through desire's illusory games and promises of a false Utopia. Of course, it cost the teacher-prophet big time to challenge its powerful, religio-political manifestations. Yet, by becoming its archetypal scapegoat, He has exposed the human predicament and revealed its solution, viz. detachment. Our realignment with Divine Source, the Non-Scapegoater par excellence, changes everything. We can now grasp something of the outflowing nature of Divine Love and our own, somewhat flawed inner workings.

The Source in which we were conceived is a giving, non-demanding divinity, One who draws us back into Union without the judgement of mankind's devil gods. Once and for all, the Healer of all healers, the Cosmic Parent, has nailed the lies of religion, politics and culture. These human fixes, the caps on violence and acquisitive desire, have been exposed for what they are; ineffective at best and hypocritical at worst. For, the adversarial *satanic* nature of the desire matrix ingeniously adapts any constraints placed upon it, morphing the very structures of limitation into powerful channels of desire contagion. In short, they don't make human society any better but rather, considerably worse. No, surely deep surgery at the psyche-soul level of each and everyone of us is urgently required; a spiritual rewiring that births us into freedom, the freedom of Return, the freedom of the transcendent Queendom.

In our 21st century world many are throwing off the old cultural constraints, as conservative structures dissolve and mimetic desire spreads rapidly through the global village via the bombardment of digital media. Is it any wonder that as acquisitive desire asserts itself as the new divinity of mankind, violence, the fruit of frustrated rivalry escalates. As the limits of desire are removed the savagery of our species increases as evidenced on our daily news bulletins. The fight of warring brothers has intensified to gigantian and deeply sadistic levels. Model Obstacles block our way, Monstrous Doubles threaten our being, the fight is on.

Sadly, Christianity in general, has missed the boat, still enamoured by its illicit affair with the power structures of man . The answer to human conflict lies under its theological nose yet it still chooses the kings of Earth rather than their scapegoats. Yeshua, bar Yosef's message of the withheld key of knowledge is as apt today as it was in Roman occupied Palestine. The dynamics of desire and violence are kept in the vaults of learning rather than proclaimed from the rooftops. The result? A pestilence of inner and outer communal breakdown, a rudderless riot that seeks out victims to ease its metaphysical pain.

I believe that it's time for the true message of the Nazarene to penetrate the raging desire matrix. Time for a new form of peace, both personal and societal. A recognition of the scapegoated God in the suffering of our scapegoats. A joyous resurrection from the death of desire bonds into the very liberty of Divine Love itself. It's an exciting time to be alive, an opportunity to let the Queendom manifest within and without. A challenge for all who bear the name of Yeshua.

Glossary

Listed below are definitions of a few key terms that are critical to the understanding of the text.

Culture = a way of thinking that has emerged to help human society cope with the violence and rivalry of skewed desire.

Culture comprises, rites/ritual, myths, laws, structures. All culture is a form of religion and all religion cultural.

Divine Love = Transcendent Source or Ultimate Reality. More than an all embracing energy, this giving Presence seeks union and relationship with all whom it has birthed.

Mimesis = the ability to copy or imitate someone outside the Self without prior conscious thought.

Mimesis is the subconscious imitative reflex with which we are equipped in order to learn from significant others, e.g. our parents during infancy. All learning comes through copying. Indeed, we are wired to receive a unique Divine *desire frequency or Will* and conform to it. However, something primal has gone wrong in our inherited mimetic settings, resulting in us regularly absorbing the desires of others, possessing them and believing them to be our very own. This dysfunctional process initiates the process of human rivalry, one which usually results in some form of expulsion or violent act.

Myths = the story of the scapegoat and its expulsion as described by the scapegoating community. Of course, the scapegoat may have another version of past events.

Psyche-Soul = the interface of Self and space-time reality.

Life in the world of form requires a go-between self, one linking the realm of spirit and the material world with all its flood of experiential and sensory input. Comprising day-to-day consciousness and the lower strata of the unconscious, this aspect of self interprets stores and interprets the events of our interpersonal interactions and desire transfers. In its dysfunctional, fragmented form I have chosen to refer to it as *ego*.

Rites/Ritual =dramatic re-enactments of the original, violent expulsion of the victim.

Sacrificial Religion = a belief system whereby a victim, either animal or human is killed in order to placate an offended divinity.

A victim of the scapegoat mechanism may, inadvertently, take on the nature of a divinity following their communal demise. If their violent departure has brought about a much sought after peace, then they're either perceived as a god, a great dispenser of peace or as one to have successfully appeased the god whose righteous anger first led to the cracks appearing within our individual life or community. The victim may even become a *devil-god*, one who causes the problems but also fixes them through their death.

Scapegoat Mechanism = the human dynamic whereby individuals and communities release the build up of desire rivalry and its accompanying tensions.

In this process a victim or subgroup is randomly chosen, to carry the blame for the flaws appearing in the psycho-social life of an individual or, alternatively ,within the greater community. Such a selection often targets a victim that somehow appears *different*. The scapegoating process usually involves a number of increasingly intense stages, e.g targeted humor, gossip, verbal and often physical violence before the *other* is finally frozen out or physically expelled from the community. This *sending away* may ultimately take the form of murder or community sanctioned killing. Once the victim has been removed a strange cathartic peace returns to permeate the community in question, thus reinforcing their belief that their social problems were indeed the *fault* of their designated victim.

Skewed Desire = a horizontal or angled desire that latches onto the desire emanating from a fellow human being.

The desire transmitter is either someone on the same *level as ourselves,* e.g. a brother, sister, friend or, alternatively, an *authority figure or model,* someone we look up to e.g. a parent, teacher, boss, sporting celebrity , film star etc.

Spirit = the higher unconscious of the Self. The image or spark of the Divine via which Transcendence flows into human consciousness and experience.

Spirit Breath = that aspect of Ultimate Reality which generously flows into, and engages with, our space-time consciousness.

Structures = Organizations and institutions that form hierarchies to let folk know their place or station within the community. e.g. family, government, courts, faith groups.

The aim of these is to enforce laws, both spoken and unspoken by means of distancing us from our desire models. The greater the distance the more unlikely we are to absorb or steal the desire of another.

Sub-personality.=.A fragment of the *psyche-soul,* broken off during an experience of trauma, particularly in infancy.

The default settings of these little, hyper aspects of the psyche-soul usually centre on defence, the prevention of further pain and inter-personal rejection. Each has its own associated emotion, which raises its energetic head on the misperceived return of the founding trauma. When not active, sub-personalities tend to rest up in packs within the barracks of the lower unconscious, eagerly awaiting the order to strike.

Queendom of God = Commonly referred to as the *Kingdom* of God within traditional Christian thought, this inner space is where we enter into mimesis with Divine Love, having disengaged from the dysfunctional effects of skewed mimesis, viz absorbing and rivaling the desire of others.

About The Author

Dylan Morrison is a spiritual author, poet and contemporary Yeshua thinker, presently living in the historic, cathedral city of Lincoln, England.

Raised in Northern Ireland, Dylan has a great empathy with all who've travelled through dysfunctional religious movements in their search for meaning. He writes to expose religious control whilst bringing hope to those who've suffered from various forms of spiritual abuse.

Dylan believes that the mysticism of Yeshua bar Yosef, the Nazarene prophet-teacher, holds the key for those searching for an authentic spirituality; one that satisfies the hunger of angst-ridden, 21st century man.

Also By Dylan Morrison

The Prodigal Prophet

A roller coaster tale of religious disillusionment and Divine hijacking

Bolts From The Blue

An out of the box inspirational reader

Way Beyond The Blue

Sayings of the Christian Mystics & more

Available in paperback, Kindle and other ebook formats

Printed in Great Britain
by Amazon.co.uk, Ltd.,
Marston Gate.